GOD'S PORCH

A 60 Day Devotional to Unlocking Your Best Life

RUSSELL L. ESTES

PREFACE

Cancer is a scary word. Hearing that word as a doctor discusses his findings with you is something that will always be etched in your memory. It stays fresh. You can recall every word mentioned. I remember hearing the words my doctor said to me like it was only hours ago. But it's not only a medical diagnosis that can cause havoc in your life, it can be anything that stands in the way of the life God intends for you. Perhaps an addiction. Maybe finances, relationship issues, or a past that you can't let go of. Accepting that these roadblocks exist is frightening. But what comes next is what defines who you are.

How do you respond? What will you do when faced with anything in life that keeps you from reaching your full potential? For most of us, we look for the best possible way to conquer our fears, and we settle for that. But God wants more for you. We all contain gifts, desires, and talents that we rarely use because we do not fully give ourselves to God.

Ephesians 3:20-21 tells us that *"**God can do anything — far more than you could ever imagine or guess or request in your wildest dreams! He does it not by pushing us around but by working within us, his Spirit deeply and gently within us.**"*

We all will face things in life that could, and sometimes do, wreck our whole life. During these times, we call upon God to "fix" our problems. But He doesn't want to just fix your problems. He wants to use them to bring out your full potential in life. But too often, we are scared to reach for what we may think is unreachable.

That's when you must ask yourself, "What are the deepest longings of your heart?" And the "more" you want in your life that you're afraid to voice out loud will remain hidden deep inside of you if you place limits on a limitless God.

Over the years, I've learned to trust God with the secret desires of my soul. And I can testify to God's faithfulness when it comes to giving me more of His vision, His presence, and His calling, all for a purpose bigger than mine.

Have you ever stopped to wonder what God's response would be to your heart's cry for more? I believe the Savior of the universe would bend down in the most caring of manners and say, "More what? And how much more? My supply is unending. My mercy is limitless. My grace is more than you need."

The more God wants for your life is beyond comprehension. That verse that I included a few paragraphs before, Ephesians 3:20-21, tells us all we need to know about what God can do in our lives: "God can do anything— far more than you could ever imagine or guess or request in your wildest dreams! He does it not by pushing us around but by working within us, his Spirit deeply and gently within us."

It changed my thinking and my life when I realized the power of this truth: God can do anything. And not just a little bit more than we dream of. Far more.

So, what are your craziest ideas, deepest longings, and grandest plans — the things you've barely allowed your soul to imagine? Because even those grand plans aren't enough. All of heaven is looking down upon you, shaking their heads and saying, "Is that all? Is that all you want? Is that all you can dream up?"

In this book, allow me to stretch your thinking, because we serve the ultimate Big Thinker. No plans of yours even compare to God's. The amazing truth is, that God can take every limitation that's been put on your life — by you or by others — and expand your heart and purpose in a way that's way bigger, way higher, and way more effective than anything you could imagine. You can never out-dream God.

INTRODUCTION

I'm a morning person. I find that the early hours of the day really offer a peace and stillness conducive to meeting with, and hearing from God. I often sit outside, watching the sunrise, and drinking coffee strong enough to make my ancestors twitch. During these times, I feel as if I am One-on-one with God. I can talk to Him like He like He is there with me... because He is.

I imagine we are sitting and watching the sunrise together. I can almost hear Him telling me, "I did that." It's not that He is bragging. He just likes to remind us that the same God who created the sunrises and universes is the same guy who put his best work into us. And that is unfathomable to try to understand how wonderful that is.

I feel as if each morning, I am sitting on God's porch with Him. I have always found that the porches of the world offer the best advice. From the overall-wearing men of generations passed, to the music put together by a group of ragtag musicians with banjos, porches have always been something that I enjoyed spending time at.

Doing my devotions early on my porch is a sure way to put God first in my day. On those mornings that I acknowledge God from the moment I place my feet on the floor, my day is different. I deal with temptation differently. I respond to difficulty differently. I engage with

God throughout the day differently. Setting aside early morning time for personal devotions lets me dedicate the whole rest of the day to God. It could help you do the same.

Making time for personal devotions and getting into the habit of daily devotions are perennial challenges for any follower of Jesus. If morning is the time you feel most "with it" and energized—that's the time to give to God. It's easy to make personal devotions just another to-do item on your list: "Okay, I gotta read so many chapters of the Bible, pray for at least this long, and write this much in my journal." However, it's important to remember that devotions are more about purpose than a specific process. Romans 14:1-9 suggests that the mode of personal devotion is really a matter of conviction. What might work well for one person may not suit another. The point of devotion is not to check off a list but to be with God.

Devotions are about inviting God's presence into your day. You might sit quietly like me, with a steaming cup of coffee, to watch the sunrise, sharing the experience with God. Or perhaps you choose to wake up by reading a spiritually evocative book. If so, ask God to join in and enlighten you. Maybe the quietness of your pre-sunrise household allows you to better heed the Spirit's leading as you read God's Word. If you need some structure, a daily devotion gets you into God's Word, helps you reflect on his presence in your day-to-day life, and leads you into prayer. Lastly, don't rush. Let your morning devotions take as long as is needed to encounter your Savior.

While a habit of daily devotions is good, it's more important to let God take the lead each and every time. Habits can be so...habitual. We just want to do the same thing again and again, as though we are following an unalterable formula. We lose sight of the purpose: to actually spend time with God. When we ask God to direct our devotions each morning, we give God the lead to set a whole different tone for the day ahead. If you're anything like me, the issues confronting the day riot through your mind from the first moment you wake. This "noise" really hinders our ability to put the Lord first. Some sound advice I've heard before is to write down the thoughts that are cluttering my mind and lift them in prayer. This way, I surrender the agenda and my mindspace to God. When we let God set the agenda in those moments, his agenda becomes the foundation for the day. Early-morning devotional time lets you get ahead of everything else and allows you to submit it all to the Lord.

Early-morning devotions give you the chance to turn the whole day over to the Lord. If you're a morning person, you can give God your best energy. Even if you don't care much for the morning, acknowledging God first thing, and asking him what he wants to do equips you to deal with the day's challenges on a more solid footing.

God's Porch is a sixty-day devotional designed to get you off on the right foot. Although it is scripture-based and packed full of God's Word, it should not fully replace God's Word, only compliment it with deep thought and inspirational stories.

I invite you to dedicate sixty days to this book. Truly invest in it. Because what you are really investing in is unlocking your full potential of walking into the plan that God intends for you to have. God's Porch was written in a format that you can spend a few minutes each day, without having to find a good stopping point. Each devotion should take no more than fifteen to twenty minutes of your time but hopefully will lead to a longer talk with God.

Sixty days. Fifteen minutes a day. That doesn't seem like a long time to exchange for unlocking your full potential and your best life. Through life stories, and lessons of compassion, love, courage, and hope, maybe something inside of you will clock. Perhaps you will have a new perspective on what life has to offer. Maybe you will learn that the limits that are holding you back were placed there only by you.

I invite you to spend a little time on ***God's Porch***. I believe something amazing is waiting for you there.

Faith and reason are often viewed as opposites. In the beloved Christmas film, Miracle on 34th Street, the lawyer Fred Gailey tells Susan, "Faith is believing in something when common sense tells you not to." While there indeed is more to faith than common sense, it is also true that faith does not ignore reason.

Throughout my life, I have believed in many things that later let me down. Things like signs that say, "World's Best Coffee." I once believed that everyone liked sweat tea, whereas I found that folks north of Kentucky did not care as much for it. I would immediately offer my condolences and prayers.

Many things find a spot in our belief-o-meter that some would argue their existence. I am not talking about things we know are real, like good cobblers and the proof of Bigfoot. But I am talking of bigger things. Things like prayers that come true, healing that happens, and miracles that will change your whole world.

Take the teachings in Acts, for example, the first noted episode of *"The Walking Dead"*

Why should any of you consider it incredible that God raises the dead? ~ ACTS 26:8

In his defense before Agrippa, Paul appealed to both personal experience and Scripture. His argument from experience focused on his former life as a persecutor of Christians. His view changed when the risen Jesus appeared to him and said that He had appointed Paul to be ***"a servant and as a witness of what you have seen and will see of me" (v. 16)***. Paul's message was not based on philosophical or theological speculation. He knew it was true because he had seen and heard the living Christ.

Yet at the very heart of Paul's defense was an appeal to Scripture. The main reason Paul changed his view was his realization that the Christian message claimed: ***"nothing beyond what the prophets and Moses said would happen—that the Messiah would suffer and, as the first to rise from the dead, would bring the message of light to his own people and to the Gentiles" (v. 22–23).*** No wonder Paul said that his message was "reasonable". Rather than being insane, as Festus asserted, the things Paul said were the sober truth. Paul had said no more than what God had already predicted in the Scriptures. Paul's claims were also based on fact. The things he spoke about were ***"not done in a corner" (v. 26).*** They had been seen by many.

Reason alone will not lead someone to faith in Christ. That is why engaging in argumentation rarely produces converts. But we also know that the Christian faith is not unreasonable. The gospel message is based on facts and the sober truth of God's Word. If you know an unbeliever, challenge them to study the Scriptures, and then believe!

Who knows, before long, they may believe in scripture as much as they do that Elvis is alive and well and living in the Bahamas. Although they'd be wrong. Everyone knows that Elvis lives in a Winnebago in Florida.

DAY 2 ON THE PORCH

Pastors are called many things. Some people address them as reverends, preachers, or even just brothers. Growing up, I remember visiting a church in a nearby town with a friend, where I recognized their pastor as someone my dad had bought a used car and a six-pack of liquid courage from. Dad called him his bootlegger, and the congregation called him Brother Fred. The term pastor comes from the Latin word for shepherd. While Brother Fred was definitely a man of many talents, this made me wonder if "shepherd" was the right word. Shepherds tend to their flock, while protecting them from the dangers of the world. Paul used this term to describe the work of the church leaders in Ephesus *(Acts 20:28).* Hoping to reach Jerusalem by Pentecost, the apostle stopped at Miletus and sent for the elders of the church of Ephesus. While he did not know exactly what lay ahead, he was certain that "prison and hardships" would be in his future.

Now I commit you to God and to the word of his grace. ~ *ACTS 20:32*

Paul's tone was grave because he knew he would not see these leaders again. He began by reminding them of his own pattern of life and ministry. The heart of his message was a charge to "keep watch" (v. 28). Like ordinary shepherds, pastors must act as guardians over God's flock.

The threat from false teaching can come from both outside and inside the church. Personal ambition is a major motive for false teachers that arise within the church. They ***"distort the truth in order to draw away disciples after them" (v. 30).*** False teachers are often motivated by greed. They enrich themselves at the expense of God's people. Using language reminiscent of the prophet Samuel's farewell address in 1 Samuel 12:1–5, Paul urged the church's leaders to follow his example instead.

The apostle's warning shows that one of the primary functions of the church's leaders is to teach God's Word. This is why 1 Timothy 3:2 says anyone who serves as an overseer must be "able to teach."

In Ephesians 4:11, Paul says that pastors whose ministry is teaching are Christ's gift to the church. Do you pray for your pastor? Pastors need wisdom from God's Word and the courage to speak the truth. Maybe you can write a note or send an email to offer your encouragement and express appreciation for their ministry.

Who knows, perhaps the very guy that you buy a used Pontiac from on Tuesday and hollers the gospel on Sunday is the one we need to pray for the most.

DAY 3 ON THE PORCH

In the summer of, at best guess, about '82 I learned a valuable lesson on forgiveness. I was around the age of ten or eleven, so the exact timing escapes me. But I remember the actions clearly. We were closing in on an event I had been looking forward to—the annual Bike-a-Thon in our neighboring town. At this event, people would "sponsor" you so much per mile to ride your bike, and it all went to a charity. I already rode my bike for miles on end daily. This would be a breeze.

Two days before the event, a friend borrowed my bicycle to ride to the store. When he got there, in hast, he laid it on the ground behind a parked truck. You can guess what happened next. The truck owner backed over my bike, leaving it crippled beyond repair. I was mad. My friend was embarrassed by his carelessness. But none of that helped my Bike-a-Thon dilemma.

Dad had been saving for a new radio for his car. The old one had gone out, and he had eight-track tapes that couldn't' holler without a new tape deck. And to my surprise, he took that money and bought me another bike from a "junk dealer" he frequented. It wasn't new, but even this used bicycle was better than my old one.

I made the Bike-a-Thon. Raised a bunch of money. My friend who had been careless with my old bike even came to support me. I forgave him. Through a bad situation, I gained a lesson and a better bike. I had been shown grace by my old man and learned a lesson in forgiveness toward my friend.

That is much the same way Salvation works. Salvation is by grace. The gift we have received from Christ is so great that we could never pay it back. And although we cannot repay this debt, we still owe something to Jesus. As the old song says, "Jesus paid it all, all to Him I owe."

Forgive us our debts, as we also have forgiven our debtors. ~ MATTHEW 6:12

In Paul's letters from prison, we are reminded of all that we owe to Jesus. Many of the Christian duties Paul emphasized in his prison letters, especially in those sections that describe the nature of the Christian life, come together in the apostle's appeal to Philemon.

Paul's request calls for sacrifice on both parts. Onesimus sacrifices his pride by returning to his old master. Philemon will lose a servant if he sends Onesimus back to Paul. Commentators are divided on whether Paul expects Philemon to free Onesimus. Elsewhere, however, Paul warns Christians not to become enslaved and urges those who already are slaves to obtain their freedom if possible *(1 Cor. 7:21–23).* Paul tells Philemon to charge any wrong that Onesimus has done or debt he has incurred to Paul's account. If there is shared loss, there is also love. Love for one another, and ultimately for Christ.

Isn't grace a wonderful thing? Isn't salvation even better? Bikes don't last forever... but these two things are tied to eternity.

DAY 4 ON THE PORCH

I start most of my mornings by giving thanks. I usually start my morning prayer in praise, telling God what He already knows—how wonderful, powerful, and great He is. I usually tell Him I am aware He is the Creator of everything, Master of all, and I admit to Him that He could out fish me any day of the week.

I think it is important to give thanks in prayer. I start naming things so fast I almost feel like a hip-hop rapper—friends, family, my career, the food I eat, nanner puddin', Nicholas Lou Saban, '69 Camaros... the list went on and on.

Throughout my life, I have been through things that some would say are no reason to be thankful for. But through it all, God has shown me how to really enjoy the things that didn't stand out before. Things like sunrises. The changing of seasons. Coffee on a cool morning. Birds singing. Old gospel music and Willie Nelson.

So often, it's easy to ask why.

"Why does God bless everyone except me?"

"Why do I have so much stress and worry in my life, while others seem to always be happy?"

Are these questions that you've asked yourself? I have... just being honest. It took me too long to realize that the secret to a happy life was no secret at all. It's not money. It's not travel. It's not retirement. It's not success as you climb the social ladder. It's the happiness and blessings that only God can give you through obedience to Him. And what helped me change my way of thinking was my way of asking.

"God, I don't care **WHY** these things are happening, but just tell me **WHAT** you want me to do with them."

Even in the bad circumstances, God can be glorified. Your faith that He will strengthen you through them will change your entire way of thinking.

Yes, I've had plenty to be worried about, but I've learned to give it to God through faith. He's blessed me, my family, ... my life, more than I ever realized I could be blessed.

We may say we have faith in God, but if we are not obeying Him, our faith is in vain. We must not only trust God, but we must step out in faith and obey Him as well. If He sends you to holler about Him in front of a crowd, don't let your shyness get in the way. You may think you can't form the right words, but if you trust enough, those words will come.

Many times, we do not obey God because we do not truly trust Him. When we obey God, we demonstrate our trust in Him. Do you trust that God knows what's best for you and desires to provide more for you than what you could do for yourself? Then choose to obey Him! He has everything under control, and He will not lead you astray. When you are walking in obedience to Him, you are in the safest place possible... the center of His will.

Have you avoided obeying God because you were afraid to trust Him? Afraid that His answer may not be the answer you want? It takes faith to obey, yet we can never see His blessings in our lives if we are not willing to obey Him. There may be some apprehension and fear, but don't let that stop you from obeying Him. Ask God to give you the strength to have faith to obey Him.

Most sermons begin with a prayer. Sometimes we are tempted to treat it as a formality, like playing the national anthem before the game. Paul saw prayer as far more. For him, it was a source of help and power.

Let your conversation be always full of grace, seasoned with salt. ~ COLOSSIANS 4:6

Sometimes when we pray, we say we are having our "devotions." But Paul urges the Colossians to "devote" themselves to prayer. The Greek expresses the idea of being busily engaged with something. Prayer is not a formality but an occupation. Furthermore, it is a demanding occupation. It requires the disposition of someone who is on guard and keeping watch. Prayer also requires a particular kind of expectation. Not the disposition of someone who makes demands but a grateful and trusting spirit that believes that God will answer in a way best suited to our needs.

Paul asked the Colossians to pray that God would "open a door for our message". This is a striking request given his circumstance. We might have expected him, as a prisoner, to ask for his freedom or maybe for justice. Instead, he asks for an opportunity to make Christ known. Paul's request reflects not only his sense of mission but also his conviction that success in preaching is dependent upon God. In addition to opportunity, Paul asked for clarity: "Pray that I may proclaim it clearly, as I should". The skill that is required to preach is also a work of God.

Most opportunities to proclaim Christ happen outside the assembly of believers. That's why Paul urges the Colossians to season their ordinary conversations with grace and salt. Grace does not mean elegant speech but the message of grace. Salt alludes to Jesus' command that His disciples be "the salt of the earth" *(Matt. 5:13)*.

You do not need to talk like Shakespeare to proclaim the grace of Christ. Nor do you need to *pretty up* your prayers. Just talk to Him. That's what He really wants. As you pray today, ask God to give you the opportunity, clarity, and courage to tell someone about Jesus. And if there's room left, tell him thanks for something amazing... like nanner puddin'.

DAY 5 ON THE PORCH

S ome mornings, I make mistakes. Sometimes, I use poor judgment and turn on the cable news. The talking heads will be hollering about how more and more people are living in fear and avoiding things they once loved. Things like amusement parks, major sporting events, and Baptist potlucks. They're afraid of viruses, violence, and undercooked pork.

This stuff does not set you off on the right foot in the morning. Negative thoughts will control your life if you let them. The enemy is constantly seeking to fill our mind with destructive and harmful thoughts—whether of fear, worry, insecurity, anxiety, temptation, envy. . . the list is longer than a Lincoln Continental.

It's all too easy for Satan to manipulate his way into a seat at the table intended for only you and Jesus, and to try making himself at home in your mind. Confidence in yourself has a valid place of importance in the life of every believer. Confidence is not so much built upon our emotions and feelings as it is on our beliefs and understanding. It is of paramount importance that we find ourselves continually reorienting our emotions when they stray from our beliefs.

Confidence derived from emotions will forever shift and be unstable. But confidence rooted in the Lord will be a steady presence and a driving force in our lives. Where we go for information reveals whom we trust. Children turn to their parents instinctively. Researchers consult the most reputable journals. Scientists use the best instruments. And look at many places in the Bible. It was important to get information from credible sources. When Ahaziah was in trouble, his choice was to consult Baal. Why did the new king consider Baal to be the best source of information about his future? Because he trusted him.

Blessed is the one who trusts in the LORD, who does not look to the proud, to those who turn aside to false gods. ~ PSALM 40:4

The story of Ahaziah, Ahab's son has always fascinated me. His introductory biography informs us that he was wicked in the ways of his father and mother, and he also behaved like Jeroboam, the king who built the golden calves at Bethel and Dan. First Kings ends there, but Ahaziah's story does not.

The division here is probably not original. It is quite possible that these two books would have been written on one scroll in ancient times. So, if you keep reading into 2 Kings, you'll see Ahaziah's story continue. Here we discover that Ahaziah was seriously injured in a fall. His injury was significant enough that he feared for his life and sought divine counsel.

Like so many before him, the king did not seek God, but instead the counsel of Baal! Even after all that had happened to Ahab, his father, Ahaziah had not learned his lesson. So, God, in His mercy, took steps yet again, to show Israel that He is in control and worthy of their undivided worship.

The angel of the Lord, spoke to Elijah and sent him to confront Ahaziah with an insightful question: "Is it because there is no God in Israel for you to consult that you have sent messengers to consult Baal-Zebub, the god of Ekron?" *(2 Kings 1:3)*. The question is penetrating.

Ahab's decision to consult Baal implied that he thought of God as unreliable, or even worse, not God at all! What do your choices say about your view of God? Do they reveal Him to be totally trustworthy? Or do they suggest that your trust lies elsewhere?

Where your information comes from can make or break your whole day. Good thing there's a ***Book*** to help you choose where to look.

DAY 6 ON THE PORCH

Most mornings, I am up early. As I begin each day and share my heart on many platforms through my writings, I usually ponder just who it reaches. Maybe, I look too intently to see My God in all things. The Word of God tells us that is how He planned it to be that all of creation would be evidence of His Glory. Everything was created through His Son, Jesus for all mankind to see and know Him.

It seems as of lately, I have become quite fond of rain. The gathering of storm clouds on spring afternoons is nothing new. In fact, it has been an annual occurrence for as many years as I can remember. Yet for some unknown reason, when the clouds rise, a sense of awe and worship begins to collect in my heart and soul. A need to cry out to the Lord, sing His Praise, and invite His Presence closer.

Perhaps I'm just getting older, and it comes with the territory. I remember my dad sitting on the porch when it rained. He would say things such as, "You can smell the rain coming. It's gonna be a gullywasher!"

And still now, whenever rain begins to fall, I remember those times when he would say that. And he would always follow with "Thank ya, God. We need the rain." I still feel the need to thank God when it rains, simply because I am tangibly overwhelmed by God's Love. The rain makes me feel like He is falling all around me and saturating my life with His Presence and all those things that He gives in such a place. This is the natural workings around me.

I know. You think I need more coffee. You're thinking I need medicine to get me back on track. I could stop right here and turn this thing around with a feel-good story of some sort or relate the Lord to some personal experience or tangible object like I often do, but not today. God is taking me deeper. He is stretching me farther. Out of ordinary circumstances and my mediocre life – His Glory is coming. No, wait it is already here all around us.

This is not about religion or the way of worship that you choose to practice in a building built by man and filled with people each week. It is not about the doctrine you have determined to be your way or the religious commitment to your church. This is about Jesus. The One who took on the form of a human being, lived a perfectly sinless life to be my example, who walked a way that I am to follow, loved unconditionally, and died brutally for me.

It is about the stone that rolled away just three days later revealing a stunning victory. It depicts a Savior not weak or wavering, but resolute in purpose who obtained my freedom and gave it back to me. That is what it is about. He is coming back. He is coming for me. Am I ready? Is my head in the clouds?

You may think I've been writing about the weather here. I haven't. The clouds I speak of, in my case, have been cancer. The clouds for others are depression, failed relations, finances, your own illness or perhaps it's a longing for something that you can't even identify, but you know is missing.

When our forecast is cloudy, we need to remember that the *Son* is still there. He's still shining and so can you.

Everything that I need is found in the Presence of God. I don't have to see it— I can feel it. His Favor is all I really need to live a prosperous life soul, mind, and body. I didn't wake up and believe it. I had to wander through a whole lot of wildernesses, live through several droughts, and fall into more pits than I care to recall. I've had so many cloudy days that I should never leave home without an umbrella. But I have discovered that in the Presence of God, there is an overwhelming love and grace like I have never known before.

So, you think all this is kind of crazy? I know I used to feel the same way...crazy Christians. Until I was broken beyond repair, had sinned beyond saving, and wandered too far to come home. When I repented, turning to find Him, Jesus was right there. He is with you. He is in every cloud you see. His favor is each tiny droplet of rain covered in enough grace to get to the heart of things.

Do not be afraid. Jesus is not coming to get you. He is coming to save you. When it rains, there is usually thunder and lightning that comes with it. People are not afraid of the water in the rain but of the storm-like conditions surrounding it. God is in control. This world is not out of control and spiraling toward destruction. Our Savior is coming to take us home. He is in those clouds that seem so foreboding. We have nothing to fear. We just need enough faith to see the *Son* through the clouds.

As surely as the LORD lives, I can tell him only what the LORD tells me. ~ 1 KINGS 22:14

Near the end of 1 Kings, we might begin to wonder if God is going to resolve the difficulties facing His people. Does He have a plan? These are questions the faithful in Israel faced during the reign of Ahab. Today's passage pulls the curtain back just a bit to give a view behind the scenes.

The word from Micaiah, the prophet of the Lord, was not encouraging. While the prophets of Baal predicted Ahab's victory, God's prophet told of his death. Micaiah described a boardroom scene in heaven. At the head of the table, sat the Lord on His throne with one agenda item. "Who will entice Ahab into attacking Ramoth Gilead and going to his death there?" *(v. 20).* Or to put it another way, "How can we get Ahab to the battlefield so that he dies?"

God would compel the false prophets to lie to Ahab. This is a fascinating scene. He was in total control of this situation. The message so rattled Ahab that he disguised himself as he rode out to the battlefield *(v. 30).* He hoped to thwart God's plan, but his clever attempts failed. An archer fired his bow at "random" and the king died. Rest assured that even when you do not see His hand, God is at work all around us.

How often do we doubt that God is really working in the difficult situations in our world, our community, and even our families? Today's passage humbles us to recognize that we serve an all-powerful God who is working all things together for His purpose. It doesn't matter if it's raining, or if the *Son* is shining.

DAY 7 ON THE PORCH

I've learned some valuable things through battling cancer. I know that God could have just taken all this away, but that didn't happen. What happened was He chose to use this cancer to help me grow closer to Him. Some of the best lessons in my life came from hard times that I prayed for God to remove... but He didn't.

I had a mountain in front of me. It showed up unannounced. If I go by the odds, statistics, and projections, I should have been planning my final cookout. They said that with my diagnosis, multiple cancers, and lymphatic involvement, the average life span is eighteen to twenty-four months. I proved them wrong. I've never felt more alive. My entire world is better than ever. I see things that I didn't notice before and each and every day is wonderful... so, so wonderful.

That mountain was placed in front of me. I was told to have the faith of a mustard seed, and God would remove the mountain *(Matthew 17:20)*. My faith has never been greater, but my mountain didn't budge. Instead, I was molded, transformed, and made better because I climbed the mountain. I endured those hard times, and I am still climbing as I look for my summit. I often wondered why God put me through that. Why is He making me go through pain, stress, and worry? He could have removed it all, but He didn't. Then one day it hit me.

God didn't remove the Red Sea through Moses — He parted it!

Sometimes God doesn't remove your problems. He makes a way through them as part of your spiritual discipline and walk. It strengthens our faith and provides testimony that can help others.

If you're going through a season of pain, consume yourself in the Word and prayer. There's a lesson being taught, and the other side is going to be much better. Faith is your friend. It would be easy to throw a pity-party when a mountain shows up in your life. It would be easy to get angry at God. But perhaps this is a season in which God chose you to do something amazing. Maybe He is using something that seems hard, to show you how beautiful life is.

When your mountain shows up, don't let your faith waver. If we choose to rely on our feelings rather than on the Word of God, we will never see the wonderful summit He intends us to see. If we shift our focus from the promises in His Word to our feelings, our faith will become unstable. But when our faith is grounded in the Word, we never have to question what God says because we stand on the truth.

If you've ever held a pity party for yourself, you aren't alone. It is easy to get so wrapped up in our own emotions and our feelings. Even worse, we can let those emotions hurt others. In 1 Kings 21, we find King Ahab feeling very sorry for himself.

You shall not steal. ~ EXODUS 20:15

After God rebuked Ahab for letting the enemy king go, Ahab returned to his palace in Jezreel. To console himself he tried to purchase a plot of land near his palace that belonged to Naboth. But Naboth wouldn't sell it, saying: ***"The LORD forbid that I should give you the inheritance of my ancestors" (v. 3).***

Ahab "lay on his bed sulking and refused to eat". His wife Jezebel took matters into her own hands. She reminded Ahab that he was king of Israel and promised to get the land for him. She did so by having Naboth killed. Why didn't Ahab just take that land? Although Ahab was king, Israelite kings were not permitted to reign the way other rulers did in the ancient Near East. In Deuteronomy 17:14–20, God declared that Israelite kings were subject to the Mosaic law just like everyone else. This meant they had to respect property rights. "You shall not steal" applied to them as well.

Jezebel was not Israelite; she was Sidonian. Jezebel had no hesitations about violating God's law. So, she had Naboth killed and stole his vineyard. Ahab did not stop her. The prophet Elijah delivered a strong rebuke from the Lord: ***"I am going to bring disaster on you" (v. 21).*** And then a curious thing happened. King Ahab repented. After such an ugly sin, it may surprise us that the Lord accepted Ahab's repentance and delayed the punishment He promised.

This shocking story teaches us about God. We see His power, His sovereignty, His knowledge, and His mercy. The mountains placed in our life that should destroy us, can sometimes be the most powerful thing to grow closer to God with. Is your mountain not moving? Start digging or start climbing... either way, God will show you something amazing along the way.

DAY 8 ON THE PORCH

"God, I can't figure out what You're doing!"

That was my immediate thought after receiving a discouraging phone call on my fiftieth birthday. A day that should be filled with cake, laughter, and good times. Instead, the doctor on the other end of the call said something that made my heart skip.

"We confirmed. It's cancer. It's not good."

Years before, God had invited me to trade my plans for His. He had whispered a promise to my heart and confirmed it through His Word, wise counsel, and prayer. Believing His promise demanded faith, I had said "yes" and followed in obedience. At first, following God's plan felt exhilarating. My prayer journal read like Mark Twain's grand tale of God's greatness. It was filled with adventure, new things, and blessings I never thought I'd see.

But then, the journey began to look different than I'd imagined. The road was filled with more potholes than I'd anticipated, and as I let God direct my steps, it seemed He was leading me to the middle of nowhere, rather than in the direction of a promise fulfilled. I didn't doubt God's presence, but I questioned His plans. ***I grew discouraged.***

My enthusiasm waned. My confidence trembled. On my good days, I felt optimistic and persistent. On my bad days, I felt angry and

23

confused. And on that evening when a phone call sank my hope, I felt helpless and stuck. I remember wondering *why*. But somewhere, deep inside, I knew that God would use this not only to allow me to grow even closer to Him but to also minister to others that were struggling.

But still... "Could You just show me what You're doing, Lord?" I begged.

I don't know how long I sat there and waited for the Lord's reply. But I do know there was no flash of lightning illuminating God's brilliant plan. No thundering voice explaining His mystifying methods. Just a quiet thought impressed upon my haggard heart: ***"Do you want a God you can explain or a God you can extol?"***

Suddenly, through my haze of fear, I recognized an uncomfortable truth: A God of infinite majesty can't be measured. A God who unleashes miracles can't be contained. A God whose love is eternal can't be explained. Perhaps that's why ***Ecclesiastes 11:5*** reminds us: ***"As you do not know the way the spirit comes to the bones in the womb of a woman with child, so you do not know the work of God who makes everything."***

God sees more than we can see. He knows more than we know. He works in ways beyond our comprehension. And if we agree to follow Him only when we understand what He's doing, we'll always stop short of experiencing His inexplicable wonders.

As I sat there in my dining room, on my birthday, with a head full of questions and a heart frayed with disappointment, I realized we had a choice. We can let the mystery of God bolster our doubt or buoy our wonder. We can drown in self-pity or stand firm and use an adverse situation to scream how wonderful God is. We can get mad at God or praise Him for what He's doing.

Abraham praised God beneath the stars — even though he didn't understand how he'd ever become the father of nations.

David praised God in the wilderness — even though he didn't understand why he was running for his life instead of sitting on the throne.

The Israelites praised God with a mighty shout — even though they didn't understand Jericho's wall would fall without a fight.

And right there... on day one of this battle... I began to praise God for the cancer because what I do know about Him is far more important than what I don't:

I know God loves me, and He'll never leave me. *(John 3:16; Hebrews 13:5)*

I know He is for me and not against me. *(Romans 8:31)*

I know God's Word is true, and His heart is kind. *(Psalm 33:4; Acts 14:17)*

Lifting my head from the dining table that day, I lifted my praises to heaven. And gradually, my disappointments shriveled in the shadow of my swelling hope. My tears dried, and I went outside. I walked to the far edge of our backyard and looked back toward our home. Before me, the world looked bright with an ethereal glow. Above me, the sky melted into a stunning swirl of pink and orange. God was painting the sunset once again. I don't understand how He does it — scattering breathless beauty across the horizon every night — but I know this: It is wondrous. Just like He is.

And I trust Him that He will use this unwanted birthday present for something so grand that I won't even know what is happening. And that's really my answer to my own question... I trust Him.

If you are discouraged, today's Bible reading is one you need to hear. We meet up with God's prophet Elijah after the victory on Mt. Carmel. What an incredible day it was! God showed up in power, and the false prophets were defeated. Then why was Elijah so discouraged?

Go out and stand on the mountain in the presence of the LORD, for the LORD is about to pass by. ~ 1 KINGS 19:11

Anyone would expect that after God's power was so clearly displayed, the people of Israel would have thrown Ahab and Jezebel out of the palace. Instead, Jezebel issued orders for the prophet's assassination, forcing Elijah to flee for his life.

When Elijah thought he was far enough away from his nemesis, he sat under a tree and lamented his existence. His response is understandable. Who hasn't been there? When faced with impossible circumstances, we ask, "Lord, I did what You wanted and I thought it would work out well, but the opposite happened. Why?!"

Elijah was so discouraged he asked God to take his life. But in the face of the prophet's doubt, we see the patience of the Lord. God fed Elijah, and gave him time to rest, before telling him to keep moving. Forty days later God met him at a cave on Mt. Sinai. After allowing Elijah to vent his frustrations, God confronted him with the truth: I have a plan that you do not know about.

God would anoint a new king in Syria, which meant God was at work beyond the borders of Israel. It meant Elijah would anoint Jehu as the next king over Israel, and Ahab would be dethroned. Finally, it meant anointing Elisha as his replacement, which meant God would not abandon Israel! If Elijah wondered who would be around to see all this, God reminded him that at least 7,000 people had not compromised themselves with Baal worship!

Faced with the impossible, Elijah felt hopeless. He could only see things from his perspective. How might you be doing the same thing in your life? Do you need God's perspective? Spend time in God's presence today. Don't ask "Why God" ... Start asking "What God". What God, can I do with this to glorify You?

DAY 9 ON THE PORCH

As a kid, I often looked like I was a runaway. I had curly, unruly hair, and was as skinny as the cane poles we used to fish with. To say the least, I wasn't the kid that would be used for the Sear's Wish Book. You would be more likely to find me in the pages of The Farmer's Co-Op. I never had the lead role in any school play. The best I could secure was playing the donkey in our church's Christmas play, but even then, my name was absent from the list of actors.

But all of that was just fine with me. I enjoyed my spot in life. It has always been a great comfort for me to realize that we are fearfully and wonderfully made and that the Lord knows us before we are born. After all, He formed us in our mother's womb. He has scheduled every day of our lives, watches over our every movement and faithfully remains with us, even when we wander far away from Him.

God cares for you now and will care for you forever. ***Isaiah 46:4 tells us "Even to your old age and gray hairs, I am he, I am he who will sustain you. I have made you and I will carry you; I will sustain you and I will rescue you."***

This verse assures me that it is not only my early years when things are going well in which the Lord is interested. He is with me every day of my life, from the cradle to the grave. He cares for me from the womb to the tomb; from start to finish - from birth to death and for every day and season in between, even the bad days... ESPECIALLY the bad days.

The Lord is not only interested in me when I can provide a good day's service to Him but at ALL times. And get this... He will "sustain me and will rescue me."

I cling to that verse often. I need to be sustained and rescued. And I am guessing that many of you do, too. And I want you to know that you're not alone. Call out to Him... He is ready to rescue you.

Be careful, or you will be enticed to turn away and worship other gods and bow down to them. ~ DEUTERONOMY 11:16

In 1 Kings 17, we read that a devastating drought had come to Israel. The prophet Elijah explains that this was ordered by God. As a result of the idolatrous practices of Ahab and Jezebel, Israel had come to believe that Baal controlled the essential elements of life: the rain, the fertility of land, man and beast, life and death. They knew the one true God, yet they had abandoned Him.

In response, God took steps to bring His people back to Himself. First, He raised up a prophet, Elijah, and second, He stopped the rain. Israel had seen prophets before, but stopping the rain was new. Yet it was a fulfillment of a threat God made in the covenant at Sinai.

The lack of rain demonstrated that God was in control of all things. They had been warned in love, now they would experience His discipline. But the Lord also provided a prophet to point the people back to Him. Elijah would call the people to repentance and faithfulness.

God's care for Elijah by providing water and bread is not only a miracle but also points to His loving care. He saw the prophet's condition and cared for him. In addition, we see the faith of the widow at Zarephath who would give the smallest bit she had in obedience to God. In return, she also witnessed a miracle—"there was food every day for Elijah and for the woman and her family" *(v. 15)*.

God's provision for Elijah and the widow, even in the midst of a drought, is a beautiful example of how He cares for us. God sees your need. He loves you. He will provide for you.

DAY 10 ON THE PORCH

"That's gonna leave a mark!"

I seem to utter that sentence frequently. Mostly the results of bad choices. I've got plenty of scars... all over. From parts being professionally removed from me because they no longer work right, to finding out you should never pick up a wild baby raccoon, I've got scars to prove my ignorance.

My dad used to tell me that it was good to have scars. "It helps you remember to not do that again," he would laugh while I would holler like a run-over dog. And I guess he was about as right as any man could be. Many scars have prevented me from repeating the poor planning I'm known for.

Over time, the scars seem to be less noticeable. They fade. They don't hurt anymore. And just like the cuts and bruises, life brings scars, too. It's not just unplanned skin removal that keeps you on your toes, but life provides us with many scars to learn from.

Some call them mistakes. It's failed business opportunities, bad financial decisions, and marriages that ended quicker than the joint car loan you took out. It's promises that didn't stick. It's letting anger control our words. It's bail money and apologies the next morning. It's addictions— alcohol, drugs, brownie sundaes.

And while some do call them mistakes... they're something else: *Life scars.*

Look, I'm not perfect. Never been accused of it... but I'm not ashamed either. In fact, I get sideways more often than I stay between the lines. I've had many occasions that I failed myself, others, and even Christ. Heck, I've even fished after my license expired. What I'm saying is... I have failed many times... over and over. I think I was born with the professional ability to fail without even trying.

But you know what? My Savior still loves me, He forgave me, and for that, I am not ashamed. I take the scars and use them. I try my best daily to make my day worthy, not only for me but those that I come in contact with. It's part of my walk... it's discipleship... it's about remembering the scars and helping others heal theirs... the best you can.

It's about realizing that you can't help everyone, but you can try to show them that you care. Sometimes, showing them your scars may help heal theirs. It's about sitting and talking to friends going through hard times. It's about telling them that you have scars, too. It's about turning your own scars into healing cream.

When we realize that our Savior above can fade our scars faster than laser removal, it tends to make everything a little easier. And when we are not too prideful to use our scars to help folks, well, our old scars still have a story to tell.

None of us are immune from making bad decisions. But you don't have to let them keep you from improving yourself. Don't let your past hold you back. Discipleship is not about doing things perfectly, it is about doing things intentionally. It is your choices that show what you truly are, far more than your abilities.

The choices we make in this life really do matter! We don't need to be perfect; we aren't expected to be. We are expected to do things the best we can. Each of us can do things intentionally by serving, loving, and caring for others. Kindness is one of the best teaching tools we have. It's easy.... and the reward is just as much yours as the receiver. I have scars, but I'm not ashamed of them... I use them. Because the best thing to ever happen to me was because of the scars on the hands of my Savior.

How about you? Have you made bad choices? Are you wise or

foolish? The book of Proverbs has a lot to say about foolish and sinful choices: *"The prudent see danger and take refuge, but the simple keep going and pay the penalty" (Prov. 22:3).* And these actions have consequences: *"The waywardness of the simple will kill them, and the complacency of fools will destroy them" (Prov. 1:32).*

We will not listen to the message you have spoken to us in the name of the LORD! ~ JEREMIAH 44:16

Even though Jeremiah was kidnapped and taken to Egypt by the disobedient Jewish remnant, his prophetic ministry continued. Through the object lesson of the buried stones, he continued to tell his people that their disobedience was sinful. Their idolatry would result in the righteous wrath of God. Egypt could not protect them, for Babylon would conquer them as well. They would never return home; instead, they would die in Egypt. But, even now, the hope of humble repentance was held out to them.

The people's response was further arrogance and insolence. We might paraphrase their response this way: We will not listen. We will not obey. We reject God's warning. We will continue doing as we please. The punishment that has fallen on us is not from God but because of times in the past when we stopped worshiping idols. They were likely referring to King Josiah's revival, which lasted from about 621 to 609 B.C. In any case, they proclaimed their loyalty to the Queen of Heaven, that is, Ishtar, the Babylonian goddess of fertility.

Bad choices have been around since the days of ancient Dollar General pyramids. But those mistakes do not have to define you. But what you do about them, most certainly will.

DAY 11 ON THE PORCH

Some mornings, I wake up with parts hurting that I didn't even know I had. These mornings were even more frequent as I went through my cancer treatments. And to my frustrations, the doctors would tell me that it is, "just part of it."

Most often, I would sit outside and watch the sunrise. I would pray to the One that could make all this go away. And honestly, I even questioned sometimes why He didn't. But as the sun would find its way over the trees that line our property, I would find comfort in the words found in my Bible. I would start reading. Then I would read a little more. Before long, I would finish my devotional, read other passages, and probably have one of the best moments of the entire day.

The cancer had ravaged my body. The treatments made it worse, it seemed. But I stayed obedient... and He hugged me. He wrapped His arms around me when I was feeling tired, weak, and broken. Did my pain go away? No, but I'm not dwelling on it any longer. Am I tired? Somedays I felt as if I haven't slept in weeks. But I was reminded that I'm not in this race alone.

We all struggle with spiritual discouragement and lethargy. Mine hits me like a ton of bricks the days following treatment. Some days our circumstances threaten to overwhelm us, and we struggle just to pray.

Many times, we just don't feel like doing the things we know we should. For one reason or another, God sometimes seems far off and unreachable. But He's not. He's right there with you.

I found myself in the Psalms many times. I love these songs and praises. David faced times like these in his life. The Psalms are filled with verses that express his despair and feeling of abandonment. Yet the Psalms also give us the key to living victoriously during the dark periods of life.

Psalm 119:89-95 ~ "Forever, O LORD, Your word is settled in heaven. Your faithfulness continues throughout all generations; You established the earth, and it stands. They stand this day according to Your ordinances..."

My circumstances or feelings have not changed how I see God. He is the same God today as He was when He hung the stars in the sky, led the Israelites through the Red Sea, and fed the five thousand.

"For all things are Your servants..."

All things, even the things affecting me right now, are God's servants. The circumstances, people, and events around me are all under God. They are His servants, designed to help and bless me spiritually.

Recalling God's faithfulness and control over everything that touches us gives us strength to walk with God even when we feel like giving up in despair. After all, our feelings and circumstances have not changed God. He is perfectly capable of sustaining us if we will only let Him. We simply need to choose to keep chasing God, despite how we feel. Choosing to stay positive might not be easy. It might even involve hard work. But only God can revive and save our soul from spiritual lethargy.

Next time you feel spiritually drained or inadequate, remember that you have a choice. You can wrap yourself up in excuses and self-pity, or you can choose to draw your strength from an unchanging God.

I am not a theologian or a scholar, but I am very aware of the fact that pain is necessary for all of us. In my own life, I think I can honestly say that out of the deepest pain has come the strongest conviction of the presence of God and the love of God.

But even if you should suffer for what is right, you are blessed. ~ 1 PETER 3:14

Pain and suffering were a regular part of the life of Jeremiah. The Babylonians had temporarily withdrawn from their siege of Jerusalem in order to fight the Egyptians. Judah experienced a brief reprieve, during which Jeremiah planned to travel to his hometown to care for family business. At the city gate, however, he was falsely accused of deserting, arrested, beaten, and imprisoned. This might have been due to his unpopular prophecies and advice to surrender rather than resist.

King Zedekiah asked Jeremiah privately for a word from the Lord, which might have been an implied invitation for the prophet to change his message to gain his freedom. But God had not changed His mind, and Jeremiah remained faithful even under these circumstances. He boldly pointed out the injustice of his imprisonment— he'd committed no crime. The king didn't release him, but perhaps out of guilt, he transferred him to a better prison.

Suffering and persecution were a theme in Jeremiah's life. For the true follower of God, suffering and persecution at the hands of the world are inevitable. When pain and hardship find you, be sure to look to the One that can change it all.

DAY 12 ON THE PORCH

Birthdays are something we should celebrate. We should feel blessed that God has given us more time to honor Him. But I have had some birthdays that left me feeling anything but blessed. I would even question what I had done to make me deserve what was happening.

My life has been a whirlwind when it comes to birthdays. When I was eight, my birthday was over-staged by my sister's wedding. I was as mad as a cat with firecrackers tied to its tail. How could she do this? Why get married on *MY* day? But then, on *HER* big day, she threw me a party. Cake and everything. She even bought me a new bike with some of her wedding money.

There's more. Twelve-years old. The day before my big day, my old man had a heart attack. My birthday wish? You're not supposed to say what you wished for. But I will say I may have had a hand in my pop making it through.

Twentieth— I blew a head gasket on my car on the way to work. I was written up. I got mad. I called my boss un-Baptist words. I had to plead to keep my job. Happy birthday!

But the big one came two years ago. My fiftieth. The big 5-0! On that day, I received a call that changed everything— "The biopsy came back. It's cancer... and it doesn't look good."

"God, I don't deserve this! I have been faithful and obedient," I screamed.

It was a battle that followed. But I've fought like my life depends on it, well, because it did. Some days I didn't know how I could keep going, but somehow, I found a way. But it wasn't as much a physical battle, as much as a spiritual one.

The enemy tried to break me. He told me things that made me think this was unbeatable. But through scripture, I was reminded of David. His faith when facing Goliath, or the lion, or any other battle he faced. He gave it to God.

I was reminded of Job and everything he went through. Joseph, hated by his half-brothers...imprisoned because of a false accusation. Nonetheless, Joseph used God's gifts to help the Pharaoh lead the people during a famine. In return, Joseph received his life's greatest blessings—an admirable job, a family, and, most importantly, reconciliation and reunion with his brothers and father.

And like these men and others, I feel strengthened through my trials. And as I still have some of the battles in front of me, believe this or not, I am thankful for the trial I'm in. It has strengthened my faith.

"These trials will show that your faith is genuine. It is being tested as fire tests and purifies gold." ~ 1 Peter 1:7

The Bible repeatedly says that God has promised to meet your needs: ***"And my God will meet all your needs according to the riches of his glory in Christ Jesus"~ Philippians 4:19.***

But the Bible also tells us that with every promise there is a condition. One of the conditions for this promise is that you have to trust Him. The more you trust God, the more God can meet the needs in your life. Some of life's most desirable outcomes have come from undesirable periods of our life. But it's the wait... the journey... that produces those moments.

When ore is tested to prove if it is gold or silver, the assayer puts a fire under it, pours acid on it, and then determines whether it is genuine. Likewise, God puts faith to the test to prove it is genuine. When hardship hits in your life, your faith will be put to the test. Will you trust God? Will you lean on Him rather than lean on your own understanding?

Will you become sweeter or bitter? James said, "Knowing that the testing of your faith…." God tests our faith so that we might know it is genuine.

I have no idea what you're going through. Maybe you're being tested in life right now. Perhaps you're thinking it will never end. Don't fall into a pity-party if you're going through rough times. Let your faith pass the test! There are rewards that await! In the darkest moments, you can still see the stars. And if you trust in those, before long, the Son will shine.

DAY 13 ON THE PORCH

When I was young, I dreamed of success being associated with a bank account. Growing up without many of the things that I had seen my friends have, I thought that would bring happiness. I would have a big house, new cars, a bass boat, take vacations, and own bicycles that didn't have duct-taped seats—it would be perfect. Why? Because that's what I thought was the picture of success. It wasn't that we were not happy. We barely scraped by a few times in my juvenile life, but we never lost our smiles. I just thought all those "other things" would bring more happiness.

Do you know what happened to that dream? I forgot about it. There was a time in my life, and I remember it like it was yesterday, when I was embraced by my Father and He handed me the free gift of salvation through Jesus without price and condition.

At first, I didn't know what that meant—not fully anyway. Was it like a membership? Do I get a jacket, a ring, or a certificate? But over time, I figured it out. I read the Membership Manual. And what I gained was success… but measured by different standards than I thought success was measured by.

It was given to me as a free coat, a mantle of His grace and His love.

It had nothing to do with me. All I had to do was say, "God here I am, a messy person with a messed-up life of my own doing, and I don't want to live my life anymore the way I am."

I can tell you this, that day God showed up big time in my life and I was under the weight of His tangible presence. It was the presence of His peace and love that I cannot put into words. All I knew was that I was being changed from the inside out. I became so happy it was embarrassing. I felt warm inside. I had never felt like that, even after taco night. And I knew that whatever happened to me was something I never wanted to forget.

It wasn't that I hadn't accepted Christ before, but I had just never GIVEN myself to Him. I had taken, but not given. And that is where the difference lived. My prayer life was one-sided. I didn't give thanks as I should, but instead, I talked to Him only when I needed something. And you know what? He still loved me and even answered some of those "*I want*" prayers.

But when things changed... wow! My life was never the same from that day onwards! It was like a huge lightbulb had gone off in my hard head. Where there had been all this darkness, now there was this light emanating from the inside out. I truly stepped out of my old life into something completely new. That is when I found the success I had been searching for. It wasn't that those other things weren't something I still desired. We all long for that vacation, right? But they didn't take precedence any longer.

Still today, I choose bologna by looking at the price, instead of thickness. I still don't have a bass boat. Nary a day goes by I don't think of something that would be fun to do, own, or enjoy, but I don't have. But I don't dwell on those things.

Once God had authority, that was my longing.... to seek Him. And you know what happened? God still gave me some of those "other things" and even more. He gave this undeserving sinner some of His blessings through grace.

The fact of the matter is, I have way more than I ever thought I'd have, and it has nothing to do with success as I measured it growing up. God has truly blessed me beyond my understanding.

My dream/goal? To serve Christ. To glorify Him through

everything I do. To help others with their needs and let Him work through me in doing it. The point is — my vision of success was based on what I saw others have, when in fact, my Savior was offering even more to me all along.

Sometimes you must let go of the picture of what you thought the perfect life would be… and learn to let God show you the happiness that you can already be living.

He who heeds the Word wisely will find good, And whoever trusts in the LORD, happy is he. ~ Proverbs 16:20

I hope today you get so happy that your innards jiggle. I hope you smile so much, that H.R. sends you to be drug screened. And above all, I hope you share that happiness with someone still looking for it. If so, you'll have a successful day.

Most people place a high value on success. We judge ourselves and others by the things we have achieved, the house we live in, or the clothes we wear. If we've done well, we feel our lives should reflect our success. But the fact is that God defines "success" differently than we do. Jeremiah is a case in point: No one worried about the judgments proclaimed in his prophecies. No one repented in response to his faithful messages. He sparked no lasting revival. His enemies openly mocked him, plotted to assassinate him, threw him in prison, and tried to destroy his writings. Yet because Jeremiah was obedient, God considered him a success.

The world and its desires pass away, but whoever does the will of God lives forever. ~ 1 JOHN 2:17

People can repent of their sins, or they can face God's judgment— bottom line! Since Jeremiah preached this message in the courtyard of the Temple, he'd walked right into the mouth of the lion! Angered, the priests and false prophets arrested him. A legal hearing followed. Jeremiah's enemies accused him of prophesying against the Temple and demanded the death penalty. They'd confused a building with God. Jeremiah's defense was that the Lord had sent him to speak the truth. He boldly repeated the message and called everyone to repent! The fickle crowd switched sides and he, as a genuine prophet under God's protection, was found innocent. He found success through the Word.

As Christians, we should not be surprised when we face

persecution. We get judged often by wanting more, and living a lifestyle where God gets what's "left over". Our faithfulness and obedience will provide everything we need to live a meaningful life. Remember, eternal success will be something worth waiting for.

DAY 14 ON THE PORCH

Not long after purchasing my first car, my best friend and I headed off on a teenage, summertime adventure. The car wasn't anywhere near being in great shape, but for $575, it got me from "A" to "B". That day, "B" was Smith Lake, some hour or so away from home. And what a fun day we had… until…

We were only a few miles away from home when something unexpected happened. The car suddenly started to shake. We cautiously looked over at one another, each wondering if the other noticed the increasing vibrations that seemed to arise out of nowhere.

We continued to drive for a few minutes, peering out of the windshield to check if the road we were traveling on was bumpy and causing the car to shake. But we saw nothing. And with each passing moment, the uncontrollable shake grew stronger. I slowly pulled into an empty parking lot and we both hopped out of the car, standing there, staring at it. Nothing was visibly wrong. We decided we were close enough to home to keep driving in the shaky car. But I silently prayed as we attempted to make it home through the now-violent shaking.

After we made it safely home, the car was later checked out by my dad, and I was told that the tie rod was broken. This meant we had no real control over the car we were driving. The front wheels were acting independently of one another, and the steering wheel couldn't properly guide them in the direction we wanted them to go. I remember my dad saying we were lucky to make it home. "The Good Lord must have been with ya," he said. Thankfully, we were kept safe, and the car was able to be repaired.

That day, I learned that there will be times when things are broken and damaged in our lives, problems that seem to arise out of nowhere, pain that we can't begin to understand, and shattered pieces we're simply unable to hold together — and through it all, God will still deliver us to our destination.

Even though life's trials can be unpleasant and unnerving, still to this day I relate that experience to a verse I lean on often:

"And after you have suffered a little while, the God of all grace, who has called you to his eternal glory in Christ, will himself restore, confirm, strengthen, and establish you" ~ 1 Peter 5:10

We can learn a few things from this verse. First, our suffering will only last for a little while. It may not feel that way from our perspective, but from God's eternal perspective, our troubles here on earth are an instant considering heaven, our final destination. The Apostle Peter contrasts our present suffering with "eternal glory" — our future glory in heaven.

Secondly, we are promised that God will do four things in us: restore, confirm, strengthen, and establish.

* Restore: to complete thoroughly; to repair or adjust.

* Confirm, or secure: to set fast; to turn resolutely in a certain direction.

* Strengthen: to make strong so as to be mobile; to move something that achieves something most effectively.

* Establish: to lay the foundation of.

The brokenness in your life is not beyond repair. God sees your suffering, and He will restore, confirm, strengthen, and establish you. He is doing all these things even in your suffering.

Before attempting to steer what's broken in the direction you want it to go, welcome God into your situation. Trust that, with Him, you can travel through life's detours, diseases, delays, and disappointments because He is on the journey with you, actively guiding you towards His plans for you.

So take heart... your brokenness has an end.

The day for building your walls will come, the day for extending your boundaries. ~ MICAH 7:11

God's covenant faithfulness means that God disciplines His people, and He responds to them in kindness and mercy. Both mercy and punishment are a part of God's love and covenant faithfulness, showing His commitment to His children. In Micah 7:9 Jerusalem finally responded to Micah's calls for repentance, though only after they had suffered under God's punishment.

God now responds to their turning away from their sin. He says that He will rebuild Jerusalem's walls and extend its boundaries. His people will not only be restored but also improved upon! ***Micah 7:12*** states: ***"In that day people will come to you from Assyria and the cities of Egypt, even from Egypt to the Euphrates and from sea to sea and from mountain to mountain."***

God not only promised the physical restoration of His people, He also promised that they would become what they always were meant to be: a haven for those who seek the Lord and want to live in the right relationship with Him. Verse 13 states that the people leaving their lands to come to Jerusalem will also function as discipline, for "the earth will become desolate because of its inhabitants, as a result of their deeds." This, again, is a clear demonstration of God's faithfulness. He blesses those who seek Him and punishes those who persist in turning from Him ***(Deut. 6:4–9).***

If your life was a car restoration project, what would be removed and destroyed before the repairs could start? Ask God to help you take a hard look at your life and invite Him to begin that work in you today.

DAY 15 ON THE PORCH

Over the last year few years, I have been through things that some would say are no reason to be thankful for. But through it all, God has shown me how to really enjoy the things that didn't stand out before. Things like sunrises. The changing of seasons. Coffee on a cool morning. Birds singing. Old gospel music and Willie Nelson.

So often, it's easy to ask why.

"Why does God bless everyone except me?"

"Why do I have so much stress and worry in my life, while others seem to always be happy?"

Are these questions that you've asked yourself? I have... just being honest. It took me too long to realize that the secret to a happy life was no secret at all. It's not money. It's not travel. It's not retirement. It's not success as you climb the social ladder. It's the happiness and blessings that only God can give you through obedience to Him. And what helped me change my way of thinking was my way of asking.

"God, I don't care WHY these things are happening, but just tell me WHAT you want me to do with them."

Even in the bad circumstances, God can be glorified. Your faith that He will strengthen you through them will change your entire way of thinking. Yes, I've had plenty to be worried about, but I've learned to give it to God through faith. He's blessed me, my family, ... my life, more than I ever realized I could be blessed.

We may say we have faith in God, but if we are not obeying Him, our faith is in vain. We must not only trust God, but we must step out in faith and obey Him as well. If He sends you to holler about Him in front of a crowd, don't let your shyness get in the way. You may think you can't form the right words, but if you trust enough, those words will come. Many times, we do not obey God because we do not truly trust Him. When we obey God, we demonstrate our trust in Him.

Do you trust that God knows what's best for you and desires to provide more for you than what you could do for yourself? Then choose to obey Him! He has everything under control, and He will not lead you astray. When you are walking in obedience to Him, you are in the safest place possible...the center of His will.

Have you avoided obeying God because you were afraid to trust Him? Afraid that His answer may not be the answer you want? It takes faith to obey, yet we can never see His blessings in our lives if we are not willing to obey Him.

There may be some apprehension and fear, but don't let that stop you from obeying Him. Ask God to give you the strength to have faith to obey Him.

Even so, faith, if it hath not works, is dead, being alone. ~ James 2:17

Have you ever been so discouraged in doing good that you felt like giving up? In Micah, we found out a little about this. Micah knew that no matter how difficult his circumstances, God was with him. While for years the prophet failed to bring about any real change in God's people, Micah refused to be discouraged: "I watch in hope for the Lord, I wait for God my Savior; my God will hear me." Even though Micah's words seem to have fallen on deaf ears, he knew that what really mattered was not the people's response but God's faithfulness.

But as for me, I watch in hope for the LORD, I wait for God my Savior; my God will hear me. ~ MICAH 7:7

Even though Micah was filled by "misery" (7:1) and surrounded by people who had rejected his call to return to the Lord, he resolutely put his hope in God. He did not look at the circumstances but kept his focus on the Lord's faithfulness. Micah was demonstrating the type of faith the author of

Hebrews writes in chapter 11:1 ***"Confidence in what we hope for and assurance about what we do not see"***. Hebrews chapter 11 is often called the "Hall of Faith" because it lists people who trusted God despite their circumstances. We read of Abel, Enoch, Noah, Abraham, Sarah, and others. They did not receive the things promised but kept their eyes focused on God and His promises. Why? ***"They were longing for a better country—a heavenly one" (v. 16)***. Notice the ending in verse 16: ***"Therefore God is not ashamed to be called their God."*** What high praise is given here to these men and women who showed faith in God even when faced with challenges! May we, like Micah and the author of Hebrews, become ever more convinced, despite what we see around us, that ***"my God will hear me" (Mic. 7:7)***.

Is your faith strong enough to get you home?

DAY 16 ON THE PORCH

"What if the doctors want to change my treatment to Chemo? If this keeps spreading, I know that's what they'll want to do. But I don't want to back out on my trust in God."

That was my thought over and over early into my cancer battle. I felt like God led me to do the immunotherapy. If I bail out now and change to chemo, is that not giving up on what God led me to? Is that not short-changing my faith?"

There are several examples from the Bible where God changed directions for His followers. God is always working on our behalf and will give us the wisdom to know when and where He is calling us. Sometimes, God takes us through things because He has prepared a lesson made just for us. When God calls us to the base of the impossible mountain, he completely means for us to climb it. He's there with us the entire way. He doesn't expect us to do it by our own strength, but to lean into his.

Once we get to the top, we will see what he wants to show us, and we will never be disappointed. God has never called me to the base of a mountain that, when I finally reached the top, I didn't stand in awe of what I was seeing on the other side.

When my mountain (cancer) was placed in front of me, I had two choices... wait for God to move the mountain or answer His call to climb it. I climbed it. God held my hand. He pulled me to the next step when I was so broken, I couldn't reach for it. My decision was made with prayer and faith. And it has been a hard, but beautiful climb.

Unfortunately, all too often, our flesh-laden idols prevent us from ever setting foot on the trail that leads up our mountains. It comes through in a desire to do nothing but preserve what we are comfortable with, rather than press forward and grow. It's about our purpose and our plan—not God's.

How do we weather seasons in life when big decisions have to be made, when we bury loved ones, change jobs, when we are storm-tossed at sea, and everything we need has been stripped away? You lose your job. You're bombing several classes. Your home feels like a battleground. You've just been diagnosed with a serious illness. Your church is in dire straits.

In seasons like this, many of us (me included) feel like we need something new — a new word from God that applies directly to our situation. In the crazy storms, the shipwrecks, the starless nights, and the sunless days, we don't know how God will save us. But we do have his promises.

And when we get to the end of our lives, we will be able to say, "I had no idea how He would save me, how I would make it to the end. But never once did he fail to keep his promise." We all know about the mustard seed. We know that our faith can move mountains. But sometimes, God doesn't see fit to move that mountain. He wants us to grow in Him. He wants us to develop a stronger relationship during the trial we are up against. He wants us to climb the mountain.

I've had to climb a mountain. I often feel as if I am reaching the summit, but there are some days that I know that I am still climbing. God didn't remove my cancer, so I kept climbing. Sure, He has the power to take every ounce of it away... the tumors, the surgeries, the financial woes, the worry... all of it. But He didn't. Instead, He reached down, grabbed my hand, and said, "Let's do this." And I've never felt closer to Him.

It may be hard to comprehend what I'm about to say, but maybe I needed this ... maybe this cancer is what I needed to push through to reach the next level in my relationship with Christ. Maybe I needed a mountain to climb, just so I could see the beauty on the other side.

Don't be discouraged if things don't go your way. Don't give up and think God didn't answer your prayer. This may be when He wants to show you something so grand, the only way He can is for you to do it together.

When your mountain doesn't move... don't just wait for something to happen...

Go over it!

But our citizenship is in heaven. And we eagerly await a Savior from there, the Lord Jesus Christ. ~ PHILIPPIANS 3:20

In a letter from Paul to the Philippians, the apostle echoes the topic found in Micah 4:5. The apostle Paul knew that struggles could accompany the Christian walk (for the apostle it even meant imprisonment!). But regardless of the suffering he experienced, Paul was determined to "press on" *(Phil. 3:14).* Paul's challenge is similar to Micah's encouragement to his readers.

While both Micah and Paul urge God's people to walk faithfully, they are aware of the realities of life. Micah emphasizes two points. First, he mentions that while Israel walked with the Lord, the people around them were walking with other gods. Just like the nation of Israel was intended to draw people to the Lord, so the church is to call people to Christ. Clearly, there is a great need for evangelism.

Second, followers of Christ must faithfully wait for the Lord's coming. As the prophet, Micah states, "We will walk in the name of the Lord our God forever and ever". Paul warns Christ-followers not to focus "on earthly things". While it is tempting to agonize over the immorality of our culture, Paul reminds us that "our citizenship is in heaven". Keeping our focus on our end goal gives us strength for the journey!

Has your journey with Christ been more like a straight incline or a series of ups and downs? Did your mountain not budge? Keep climbing. The view from the top will be amazing!

DAY 17 ON THE PORCH

A few years back, I spoke to a group of college students. These were enrollees at the University of Alabama. I was pumped with pride to just be there. These students had futures so bright that after ten minutes with them, I had burnt a hole plum through the retinal tissues of my eyes. Another five minutes... total solar retinopathy.

The director introduced me to a group that seemed to have lost their pulse. I was seriously concerned for a few. I came to the podium for what seemed like a funeral. I started off by telling them about myself. Silence. Not even a golf clap.

Next, I told them about my books. Notta. Nothing. I then smiled big, took a big breath, and yelled "Roll Tide!" The place came unglued! I received applause, a dozen return "Roll Tides," and two "Yee haws."

The University of Alabama has an amazing way of building future world changers. They have graduated astronauts, award-winning engineers, and inventors of low-fat mayonnaises. Pulitzer Prize-winning author Nelle Harper Lee, who most notably authored 'To Kill a Mockingbird,' called this place home. There are doctors, lawyers, entrepreneurs, and inventors that have left their mark here.

And somehow, here I am— winner of the fifth-grade 4-H safety cartoon contest and two-time qualifier for the Freewill Baptist Vacation

Bible School ice cream eating contest. Outside of that, my most noticeable achievement was peeing over the hood of my dad's Nova. I haven't had that kind of back pressure in over thirty years, and still, here I am.

The kids I talked to had accomplished more before breakfast than I would all day. It's amazing how smart they are. It's even more amazing that I'm here. It's just not normal. But we live in extraordinary times. I guess it's fitting that someone with so many shortcomings should be at an institute of higher learning advising on making smart choices and enduring the challenges of life.

I guess it makes sense that they would have someone like me here talking about perseverance. I have absorbed and overcome so many challenges in my life that extraordinary should be a common word in my Southern vocabulary. But here's the truth… I don't do good with anything with more than five syllables. But extraordinary is the only way I can explain these times we live in, such that we can be placed in a position of having to choose between the right thing to do and secular expectations.

Kids nowadays have no choice but to be extraordinary. Anything less and they become a politician, bootlegger, or a hip-hop country singer. These kids are so confused by what we tell them will build success, that they give up on their dreams to live someone else's.

"You better do this, or you'll be in trouble… but if you do, you'll be in bigger trouble."

How can you know what to do with so many people telling you what is right? Under normal circumstances, laws are in place to make us do right. But we haven't seen normal circumstances since the last episode of Andy Griffith. The world went slap stupid after MTV was invented.

Other things were discovered that made us upright humans get sideways. Good things were removed. Like family dinners, Schoolhouse Rock, and Fonzie. Playing board games with the family was replaced with video games and conversations with A.I. Those were good for a while, but now, you couldn't find a Nintendo Duck Hunt game if you hired an investigator. They've been replaced with games to help you learn to steal cars.

People tell us that our governments are supposed to stop the damage fallen men do to each other through the implementation of laws. They say that to prevent bad people from buying a gun, we need more laws… because you know, bad people follow laws. These laws, if they are just, are intended to either hinder disordered behaviors or punish them appropriately when they are committed. The only problem is, that they go get their free glamour shot down at the local Free Night's Stay Inn, and they're out before a government-issued breakfast is served.

I'd say we have enough laws telling us what to do. It's the policies of how we enforce them that's the issue. Why do violent repeat criminals get to eat beside my family at Chuck E. Cheese while awaiting trial? I'm all about "innocent until proven guilty," but at some point, that "repeat violent criminal" part needs to have consequences, and "free while awaiting trial" shouldn't be one of them.

We don't need new laws about what we can and can't do. We need new laws to help judges keep people who want to hurt my family, steal my car, and clone my Facebook grounded until things are sorted out. It's the justice system that needs our help, not "we the people". We can make new laws all we want. We can tell others about what we are supposed to do, but we have a long history of ignoring them.

Remember when we were kids? We would get told stuff all the time that we ignored.

"Don't go barefoot when you ride your bike. You'll lose a toe… or worse."

That one never worked. My toes are so bent up from bike riding that I have to buy shoes two sizes too big.

Don't throw rocks at each other. Don't climb on top of the house, or pick up that dead bird. Don't play tackle football in the yard, you could break something. Don't walk on the grass. Don't pick the flowers. Don't pee over the hood of your dad's Nova.

Don't be the baseball pitcher unless you want a concussion. Don't get in a fight, you'll never have friends. But if you don't fight to defend your friend's honor, what kind of friend are you? Don't eat too much candy. You'll get diabetes. Don't eat fried chicken unless you want to buy cholesterol pills for the rest of your life.

None of that stopped us. You know what did? A belt. My

hindquarters had my dad's name across it on many occasions... so did his leather belt.

Our moms were more forgiving. They believed in us staying in our rooms until we learned our lesson. I once stayed in my room the whole fourth-grade year. Coincidentally, that was the year I received a BB gun for Christmas.

But like I said. This ain't nothing new. This goes back to the biblical days. It was quite easy for a Jew or Christian to find themselves at odds with the laws of that time. In some cities, to do business in the public markets, the only places to purchase food, textiles, Reese Cups, and other necessities of life, was to offer a small sacrifice to a particular pagan deity.

This was most often in the form of a small pinch of incense, or some fine cloth, perhaps your Netflix login. For Christians and Jews, even the offering could be deemed law-breaking. If you offered less than what the asking price was, it could be thirty days in county lockup and shaming by placing your picture on Facebook. Such an act was unthinkable. So, navigating the laws could be very tricky for believers in the one God of the Bible.

And it hasn't got any easier. We still don't know what to do. Don't watch Clint Eastwood movies... you'll want to punch somebody. Don't eat Mexican food one hour before bed unless you want stage four heartburn. Don't cuss. If you do, not out loud. If nobody hears you, it doesn't count anyway. Don't drink anything somebody else has to purchase for you. It causes hangovers. Don't shop shirtless. Don't cook bacon in your underwear. For Pete's sake, don't talk about God in public. You'll end up getting kicked out of the school, a club, work, and the AA meetings.

H.O.A. folks even get in on the action. Don't use colored Christmas lights. Don't park on the curb. Don't cut your grass too short. Don't plant begonias by your mailbox. Even the things we were taught growing up that we thought were respectful, can now get a guy slapped.

Don't hold doors open for girls, don't offer to carry her three hundred shopping bags like a pack-mule hiking the Grand Canyon. Don't offer to pay restaurant tabs. Don't compliment a lady. This is no longer acceptable behavior. What was once called being a gentleman is now utterly disrespectful. It gets filed under sexism.

See where I'm going. There are laws, rules, and things we just know to do. There are penalties, enforcements, and time-outs. We are expected to not buck the system. We are told to keep our mouths shut. Just sit yourself in a corner and post about it… but don't do anything about it. Just watch the cable news. Let the suits tell you how afraid you're supposed to be.

I just know that the day I was in a room full of kids smart enough to do my taxes, all I could tell them was the three things that have got me through life.

1- Keep God first and pray to Him often.

2- Do what's right, even if it's not the popular thing to do.

3- When in doubt, yell "Roll Tide!"

My son, do not make light of the Lord's discipline. ~ HEBREWS 12:5

Our relationships with others and how we act are a direct reflection of our relationship with God. Israel's leaders had not quite learned that lesson, for they remain convinced that God was among them, even looking "for the LORD's support" in their evil maneuverings. However, God did not support these leaders, and He told them clearly that their oppression of His people would actually lead to the destruction of the entire nation. Rather than God supporting and protecting them in their sin, He would judge them and cause Jerusalem—a reference to the whole nation—to be "like a plowed field" and a "heap of rubble".

Despite the discomfort we may have when reading God's judgment, this promised destruction is actually an important indicator of His love. First, it shows that God remains faithful to Israel's leadership to love them as His children, which in this case means fierce discipline. Second, God's judgment shows that He remains faithful to love the people whom these leaders are oppressing. Rather than leave them to fend for themselves, God promises that He will intervene on their behalf.

Sometimes we may act like we are above the law, that God is on our side no matter what we do or how we behave. Perhaps following the rules is part of God's entire plan. And if you ever feel in doubt… remember: ***Roll Tide!***

DAY 18 ON THE PORCH

As a young boy, it took a lot to scare me. I didn't know fear. I would climb trees so high the tops would begin to break. I'd be the first inside an abandoned house that my friends swore was haunted. I'd jump the biggest ramps we could make on a bike that was made from hand-me-down parts.

I was as brave as any kid I knew. Most of the time. But then, there were times I was so scared I'd be plum embarrassed if my friends knew. I'd lie in bed and feel so scared I couldn't catch my breath. And sometimes, I didn't even know what I was afraid of.

But when I knew, it scared me to the point I would call for the Good Lord to just go ahead and take me. I was afraid. Plain and simple. Afraid something would happen to my family. Afraid I would let them down. Afraid I wouldn't be enough for them.

I was afraid I would be a failure. I grew up without a lot of anything. I thought all shoes came already broken in and jeans were supposed to be too long, faded, and have a patch on at least one knee. I didn't know any better until I was older. And then, I wanted better for my family whenever that time came. But I was scared I couldn't provide that. I was a nobody. "Nobodies" don't have better things.

To tell the truth, I was more afraid of the things I couldn't see. I wasn't afraid of bullies, strangers, tornadoes, ghosts, snakes… nothing. You can see those things. It was failure, sickness, worry… and yes, death that scared me so bad I lost sleep and weight.

Fear has a way of taking over. It finds a crack and slips in. At night, I'd wonder if death was going to swallow me whole. I don't even know why I was so scared of death when I was young. I had always been told that the other side of death was something peaceful and pain-free. But still, there were times I lost sleep thinking about dying.

I remember as a kid, possibly around the age of twelve, my friend dared me to jump from a bluff into dark water. It was an old strip pit pond. It was probably only thirty feet or so, but to a kid looking down, I felt like I was jumping from an airplane. I got to the edge and looked over. I inched up, so close that loose gravel fell into the water below. Then I backed up.

"You chicken?" My friend hollered.

I moved back to the edge and looked down. Lord, it must have been a two-thousand-foot drop.

"Go on," he shouted. "I double dog dare ya." He was such an inspirational speaker, my friend was. He then made the clucking sound of a chicken indicating that he was going to let it be known in school that I was a big wuss. The double dog dare took me to the edge, but the sound of that clucking produced more bravery in me than a fifth of whiskey did for my underage cousins.

I inched back up. I looked down at the water. I imagined me free falling for at least twenty-five minutes. I asked God to give me the courage. I turned around, looked at my friend, and smiled. Then… I jumped!

It was terrifying, but I did it. And it did something to me. I escaped into a world where failure was no longer a word. I lived in the moment. Neither of us said much. He couldn't believe I actually did it. I couldn't either. But I did.

Why was this so hard for me to do? I wasn't scared of heights. I could swim. Why couldn't I just be fearless without being involved in chicken noises?

Seeing me do it, my friend followed suit. He splashed down like a watermelon falling from a watermelon tree. We splashed and swam for hours. We laughed and shouted and hollered like we had just won the state championship. We escaped! We lived! And you know what else we did. We proved we were not afraid!

It didn't change my life, but that day, I did feel something. I wish I could tell you that I felt less afraid, but that wasn't it. I felt sort of strong. And sometimes, feeling strong can make fear easier. Being strong. That counts for a lot. The more you go through in life, the stronger you get. And that experience takes the place of fear.

I don't know where you are right now, or who you are, or what kind of fear you're going through. You may be battling your own cancer. It may just be called by another name… like depression… anger… a failed relationship… financial hardships… it could be anything that has pushed you to the edge. And you're standing there. You're looking down at the water. You want to jump, but you're afraid. But don't forget how strong you are.

Whoever dwells in the shelter of the Most High will rest in the shadow of the Almighty. ~ PSALM 91:1

In the Psalms, we see a realistic description of these threats, but also a strong reminder of God's loving care and protection. Psalm 91 is a profound call to trust in God, even in the midst of danger. The Psalmist declares that the safest place in the world is to dwell "in the shelter of the Most High" and to "rest in the shadow of the Almighty". Because of this, we do not need to fear "the terror of the night, nor the arrow that flies by day". These real dangers are not beyond God's supervision.

Some of the most profound statements about God's protection are found in this psalm (worth bookmarking in your Bible!). The Psalmist declares that ***"no harm will overtake you, no disaster will come near you" (v. 10)***. Our daily experience may seem to indicate otherwise. Indeed, many of the godliest people in the Bible experienced persecution and suffering. So, how are we to understand this language? Perhaps it is best understood as referring to God's ultimate defeat of evil at the return of Christ. Writing from a prison cell and close to death, Paul uses similar language: ***"The Lord will rescue me from every evil***

attack and will bring me safely to his heavenly kingdom" (2 Tim. 4:17).

It is easy to look at our circumstances and experience fear. But the Psalmist and Paul looked to God for protection. This psalm is a good reminder to us that nothing can separate us from the love of Christ.

DAY 19 ON THE PORCH

He had put his foot down! His mind was made up and there was no changing it! Dad had made it perfectly clear — "You're not getting a puppy!"

Ten minutes later, me and Mom were on our way to get that puppy.

Only two remained. Eight puppies were ready for their new homes, and six had found them. They were going like fresh tomatoes at a yard sale. They were beagle mixes. Floppy ears... big eyes... tricolor! Just the kind I wanted. One was jumping around like a squirrel on Red Bull. It was hollering and howling and just calling for me. It broke free from the pen and ran toward me, tugging on the hem of my jeans.

"I want this one, Mom! Can we get him? Please?" He was perfect!

"Well, he's spoken for. But I do have this little girl here left," the older man said pointing to a smaller pup lying near the back of the pen. I went closer and looked at the pup. Standing over her, I noticed that she only had part of one of her front legs.

"She's got a gimp leg on front. Was born like that, but she's doing really good. She's the runt. Didn't think she would make it, but she's proved me wrong," the older man told me.

I looked down at her again. She was shaking in fear. I bent down to rub her. She lowered her head, cowering down and shaking more. I gently started rubbing her head. She shook less. Her tail even started to wag. She looked up at me—her big puppy dog, sad eyes looked into mine. That was all it took.

"I want her mom!"

"You sure?" Mom asked. "There'll be more pups to choose from later."

I picked her up and she started licking me in my face, causing me to laugh. "I'm sure, Mom. She's perfect!"

The older man reached over and rubbed her head while I held my new pup. "She will make you a fine pup. She's just a little ... different."

She became the best dog a kid could have. She was just a little... different.

Different. Isn't it great that we are different?

A few years back, I pulled into a job site. My radio was on a local country station. As I got out of my truck, I heard the radio playing from the construction crew. It was classic rock. *The Eagles* were reminding us about "Seven Bridges Road".

On the same site, a group of Hispanic roofers were getting after it. They were nailing so fast it sounded like machine guns. Their radio played an upbeat tune from a mariachi band. Guitars, violins, trumpets, maracas, and nail guns made for an interesting sound. It made me smile. It was... different.

Even a lunch meeting once reminded me of our uniqueness. A young lady who served us had bright red hair on one side. The other side was shaved clean down to her freckles. Her nose had a hoop in it and her lower lip had three. Forty years ago, when I was growing up, we never would have seen this. But times have changed. Times are different.

She was one of the nicest waitresses that's ever poured my sweet tea. She smiled often. Big smiles. Her personality made it easy to smile back. She chatted with us. She told us about her classes at the nearby college.

"I'm gonna be a nurse," she told me. "I want to feel like I'm making a difference."

My tip confirmed that she made our lunch enjoyable. She was pleasantly... different.

Just think of all the different people that God made. Different countries produce different people. We have different races, looks, and colors— all in God's image! There are hundreds of different languages. Even more, if you count "Southern" and "Yankee".

I'm always amazed when I think of how God created a world that's filled with incredible diversity and variety. There are different kinds of colors, tastes, sounds, foods, scenery, animals, ideas, types of leisure... the list just goes on and on. But one area that is especially intriguing to me is the variety of people God has created. In fact, everyone is different. There are no two of us alike. We are each special.

But despite our great diversity, the Bible says that we were all created in the image of God. Therefore, we all have some things in common, things that make up our 'humanness.' Just imagine—we are all the same, but... different.

Knowing that we are unique should humble us. It should make us realize just how much God loves us. We understand that no two people have the same fingerprint. That blows my mind just to consider that there is no other one in the human population who has the identical pattern that I have, or you have. It doesn't end there. We are told that one's DNA is strikingly different as well. No two people have the same DNA.

The importance of it all is quite simple, even in a complex diversified world — we accept that we are different. It never means that we must conform to the likes and looks of others, but we can accept the differences and show kindness.

Even the runt of the litter with a gimp leg can prove that we need to look beyond appearance and see that God made us unique for a reason. And I can find that so fascinating that I'm in awe of it. And I know that all I have to do is just be nice to everyone... different or not.

What comes into our minds when we think about God is the most important thing about us. This is a profoundly true statement. What we believe about God changes the way we think about ourselves, others, and the world we live in. Just like our relationship with other people, our knowledge of God is not a static thing. It grows as we get to know Him better. Even when we are all different, He wants us to be more like Him.

I keep asking that the God of our Lord Jesus Christ, the glorious Father, may give you the Spirit of wisdom and

revelation, so that you may know Him better. ~ EPHESIANS 1:17

In Ephesians 1, Paul prays for the church. His deepest desire is that we "may know him better". Paul understands that our first calling is to remain in fellowship with God. God is unlike anyone else. He created the universe and stands outside of it. The only way we can know God is because He has made Himself known to us. He is revealed through His Word and ultimately through the Lord Jesus. Paul prays that we would learn about God through the enabling power of the Holy Spirit.

God provides many pictures in Scripture to help us understand His character and attributes better. We looked at how God is like different aspects of the created world—light, water, fire, and shield. We considered passages where God is compared to animals—a lion, eagle, or bear. We examined different human occupations that illustrate aspects of God's character—shepherd, king, warrior, judge, and farmer, to name just a few. Finally, we looked at the most intimate pictures of God as a parent and husband.

Isn't it a wonderful thing that a God that can create so many different things, finds it at the top of His wish lists that we are made in His image?

DAY 20 ON THE PORCH

I magine your favorite piece of art. Is it *The Starry Night*? Maybe *The Last Supper*? What *about American Gothic*? Perhaps it's something your kid painted. It might be hanging on your fridge right now. Simple stick figures and giant flowers, or something from *Bassmaster* magazine. Maybe it's a portrait of a loved one... someone memorized in oils and canvas.

Got it? Do you have it pictured in your mind? Now imagine it painted on a piece of glass. From one side, it's beautiful. You see every brush stroke, perfectly blended to the next. It's beautiful. But flip it over. You see the back side of it. It's hard to make out any of it. Different colors are going everywhere. It's a mess!

Life is much like artwork. From one side, not a single stroke of paint is out of place. It's magnificent. But what people don't see is everything that it took to get there. People don't see "your mess." And sometimes, it's hard for us to realize why we even need the mess to have something beautiful.

John 13:7 Jesus replied, "You do not realize now what I am doing, but later you will understand."

When a loved one is sick, and you are drowning in fear, or when you're doubting God's goodness because if He was good, how could all of this be happening? What about when your marriage is falling apart, and you don't know if there is any hope... I could go on and on. Our lives are full of messes— brush strokes out of place. These are the messy moments of life. The ones that feel like they could wreck you, or that they might bury you alive.

They force us to confront our beliefs, maybe for the first time, maybe for the hundredth time. It forces us to admit that maybe when it comes to what we say we believe about God, we're frauds. Maybe we hear it in church... even post it on Facebook... but do we believe it? It forces us to see where our trust lies. It forces us to face what we believe we can expect from the God we call our Father, Healer, and Physician.

But we are not alone. He meets us in the mess. And His feelings for us do not fluctuate and do not change. He doesn't leave us there. It's typically not our first reaction to run to God when we are struggling, but it can be. And if we give Him the mess, He knows how to redeem it. It might not be in the way we want Him to.

But it could be even better. It's in the mess that we need Him the most, and He is more than willing to meet us. We are growing in these messes. Our paintings are becoming beautiful, and we don't even realize it.

Use the messy moments as an invitation to really experience His love and grace. Let Him help you paint your picture. God is doing some behind-the-scenes work. He is preparing to unleash His limitless power in and through you! It's hard to see sometimes and even harder to feel what's going on. But, trust me, it's going to be beautiful.

I hope one day you look back. I hope you realize how far you've come. I hope you see your painting from the other side. Maybe then, you'll see how good things, bad things, and sad things join to make a breathtaking portrait. And when you see this, look to the heavens and smile. The Artist will be glad you trusted Him.

Michelangelo was perhaps the greatest sculptor in history. When asked to describe his craft, he said, "Every block of stone has a statue inside it, and it is the task of the sculptor to discover it." Artists take materials in the world and reshape them to create something new. Today, we are viewing God as an artist. But, unlike Michelangelo or any ordinary artist, God is not dependent on using preexisting material. He can create from nothing!

The heavens declare the glory of God; the skies proclaim the work of his hands. ~ PSALM 19:1

In Psalm 19, David proclaims: "The heavens declare the glory of God; the skies proclaim the work of his hands". David looks up at the night sky and is awestruck by God's handiwork. When we take the time to really look at the universe God made, from the smallest blade of grass to the largest supernova, we cannot fail to see God's grandeur and His artistic prowess. Even though nature cannot speak audibly, it communicates to us who God is.

God's artistry is also seen in Scripture. God's Word is "perfect" and "refreshing to the soul" *(v. 7)*. His commands are "radiant" and "pure" *(v. 8–9)*. They are designed to help us grow in wisdom and bring "joy to the heart" *(v. 7–8)*. God's Word is not only true but also beautiful. God inspired the writers of the Bible to pen gripping narratives and majestic poetry. As David reflects on God's Word, he realizes it is "more precious than gold" and "sweeter than honey" *(v. 10)*. The artistry in Scripture reflects God's nature as endlessly creative.

David desires that his own words and thoughts would be true and beautiful like God's. He prays, "May the words of my mouth and this meditation of my heart be pleasing in your sight" *(v. 14)*.

Take some time today to look around at the world that God created. Where do you see evidence of God's artistry? As you read Scripture, notice the beauty and the truth contained within it. It may seem like a mess now, but something beautiful will come of it.

DAY 21 ON THE PORCH

Have you ever been so sick that you felt like a flat possum on a busy two-lane road? I have. Too often, I've been in emergency departments laying on beds at the same temperature as an ice cream cooler. Sometimes, it was flu, pneumonia, or another virus. Then the cancer battle—that one kept me feeling so bad that some days I would not even attempt to move. When my kidney tried giving up the spirit to go be with Jesus through the Pearly Gates of the nephrology ever after, that was a new level of "feel bad". I had to listen to motivational speakers before I attempted to stand.

But I'm a certified, red-blooded, southern, blue-collar, tough-as-nails Man! (notice the capital "M") And dadgummit... I do what those types of men do — I remind my wife every fifteen minutes how bad I feel. I moan in tones that make the dog tilt its head and stare at me. I move slowly. I try hard to work up the strength to start calling my closest relatives.

And during those times, I would get messages from folks. If I hadn't put out any new material in a few days, people would become worried. I apologized often for not responding to everyone, but I didn't check my phone like I did when I still had a pulse. When I was at my sickest, I would try to write a new column for folks, and each time it turned into my obituary. I was convinced this could be it.

If I could have eaten, I knew what would cure me. It's been the miracle cure my entire life. What I needed was comfort food. I remember being a kid and Momma would make chicken and dumplings that could cure Ebola. She would fill the kitchen with so much steam that the wrinkles would come out of the curtains. The aroma itself would make your fever go down. Neighbors would open their windows just for a whiff.

That type of culinary war against a school excuse note was about as close to eating at a table in Heaven as you could get. Even if I felt as bad as a catfish on a trot line, a bowl of Momma's chicken and dumplings would have me back jumping ramps on my pieced-together bike in less than an hour.

Dad was the same way. He needed a prescription from Mom's kitchen to keep him above dirt. But his elixir was slightly different. The "go-to" comfort food always seems to be soups and stuff you eat from a bowl. But Dad needed something that would clog arteries to make him feel better—fried chicken livers and biscuits and gravy were his prescriptions. When that came out, I knew Daddy was down. But after two plates, he was a new man. When he would smell the grease heating up, he would come off his deathbed and start eating like a prison camp survivor.

I'm not sure how many generations it was passed down from, but comfort food cooking is a carried gene. Momma must have carried it from both sides of her family. She believed in the gospel according to whole milk and in the healing properties of banana pudding. And most Southerners do. When someone passes away, we bring food. When a neighbor catches a cough… more food. I've seen porches collapse under the weight of funeral casseroles. My buddy's transmission went out a few weeks ago. I took him out for barbecue. He thanked me and shook my hand so hard my shoulder dislocated.

And why? It's just what's right! It comes delivered by concerned Baptists and Methodists who stack Piggly Wiggly bags on porches. We think that calories and bacon grease were what Jesus used to raise Lazarus. Even teenage girls cure breakups with Ben and Jerry's.

Maybe comfort food is what we need. I don't remember being sick too often when we used to get government cheese from a delivery van. Maybe that is part of the answer. I don't know. But even with the comfort food, I do know that the biggest part of our healing doesn't come from a crockpot. It comes from a Higher Power.

When we place our healing into the hands of the great Physician, that's when true healing begins. And it can cure more than what a medical diagnosis can put on paper. It can cure brokenness, emptiness, and a whole list of other things that life throws at us.

The first step toward healing is recognizing that you are sick. Aspiring medical students are often counseled to minor in psychology. The reason for this is that treating someone medically involves more than simply diagnosing diseases and prescribing treatments. The patient also must accept that they are sick and that the treatment offered will help them.

I will heal their waywardness and love them freely. ~ HOSEA 14:4

The prophet Hosea ministered to Israel during a time when the nation was prosperous and thriving economically. But while their pocketbooks might have been healthy, their hearts were not. They worshiped idols and oppressed the poor. God raised Hosea to warn them of the danger they faced if they continued this path. In Hosea 14, the prophet's final plea to the nation was: ***"Return, Israel, to the LORD your God. Your sins have been your downfall!"*** *(v. 1).*

Israel's sin was like a sickness eating away at the nation from the inside. First, they needed to be honest about their condition. Instead of trusting in God and worshiping Him alone, they had often trusted in alliances with Assyria and worshiped idols *(v. 3).* They had ignored God's command to care for the orphan and the widow. There could be no forgiveness and no healing without accepting their guilt and turning to their God.

God assured Israel that if they would repent, He "will heal their waywardness and love them freely" *(v. 4).* God is the great physician. He is able to heal physical sickness. And He alone could heal the spiritual sickness that Israel had brought upon itself. God could not only restore Israel, but He could also cause the nation to thrive *(v. 5–8).*

Perhaps you have struggled with a recurring sin in your past or continue to do so in the present. Turn to the Great Physician! ***"If we confess our sins, he is faithful and just and will forgive us our sins and purify us from all unrighteousness" (1 John 1:9).*** Through Christ's death and resurrection, we can experience true healing. That and a bowl of chicken and dumplings, and perhaps an episode or three of Andy Griffith, and you'll be back to doing yard work before the dandelions take over your yard.

DAY 22 ON THE PORCH

Facing the giants of every day can be grueling. From illness to finances to mental disease, it takes a toll on you. I've had so many giants show up in my mailbox, that I've had to reinforce it to keep it from being lopsided. At times, the medical bills would pile up so much, they were being delivered by a U-Haul. But even with the financial burden that comes from long-term illnesses, the real giants are the ones that live inside of us. The ones that attack us when we are weak. Finding strength in all this seems far-fetched, but not if we look in the right place.

I'll be the first to admit... I'm battle-worn. Some days I feel weary. Almost every day, fatigue wins. But somehow, some way, I get up the next day and keep on smiling. That "somehow, someway" is God.

Phil Wickham sings a perfect song for this called "Battle Belongs", referring to 2 Chronicles 20 where the people of Ammon and Moab stood up against the inhabitants of Mount Seir to utterly kill and destroy them. This chapter describes how God set ambushes against the enemies of Judah. It's a story of this huge army that is amassed to come against the people of God. And with Him on their side, His people are victorious.

♪♪ When all I see is the battle, You see my victory

When all I see is the mountain, You see a mountain moved
And as I walk through the shadow, Your love surrounds me
There's nothing to fear now for I am safe with You
So, when I fight, I'll fight on my knees
With my hands lifted high
Oh God, the battle belongs to You
And every fear I lay at Your feet
I'll sing through the night
Oh God, the battle belongs to You♪♪♪

This also reminds me of another circumstance where God intervened and let the impossible become possible. The account of David versus Goliath is one of the most well-known stories in all of the Bible. But instead of focusing on David's story, we should focus on God's story. Don't get me wrong, many of the traits that David has, we can learn from, but this was God working through him. David did something impossible without Him.

David was brave, but he had more faith than any of the other warriors. In his battle against a giant, his mere strength would not stand a chance, but his strength came from the Lord. I want to be like David. I want to be strong enough to say, "God, I can't do this without You. The battle is Yours."

Whether it be physical, emotional, or spiritual, and you come on your own with just some sticks and a stone, here's what's going to happen. You're going to get your teeth kicked in. That Goliath is going to step all over you and he's going to destroy you because on your own as a human, you can't defeat Goliath.

The one stone that matters is David's faith in God. It was the faith that David had in God that sparked his righteous indignation to stand up for God's name when no one else would. God gave him the courage to face the Goliath which he could not win on his own. David had to trust his Heavenly Father more than men.

It will be God that delivers you in the darkest times of your life. God's warriors saw the victory, not because of what he had on the outside, but because of who he had on the inside. It's not about your mental abilities; the fatness of your bank account; your athletic prowess; or your good looks; none of that matters. What matters is who you have on the inside. When you trust in Christ completely, he can give you the courage needed to face any challenge for his glory. The battle belongs to the Lord.

Throughout its history, Israel was in an almost constant state of warfare. During the events described in the Old Testament, they were attacked by the Egyptians, Philistines, Moabites, Assyrians, and Babylonians—to name just a few enemies. In such a dangerous world, warriors were both common and necessary.

The LORD is a warrior; the LORD is his name. Pharaoh's chariots and his army he has hurled into the sea. ~ EXODUS 15:3–4

In many places in Scripture, God is described as a warrior. In Exodus 15, Israel had achieved the unthinkable. They had escaped from Egypt, the most powerful nation on earth at the time. They did not escape because of their military prowess or their political savvy as negotiators. Instead, they were freed from slavery because God fought on their behalf. After the Egyptian army drowned in the Red Sea, Moses led Israel in a hymn of praise that proclaimed: ***"The LORD is a warrior, the LORD is his name" (v. 3).*** He silenced the prideful boasting of the Egyptian army. God showed that He is unique. There is no one like Him. Egypt's gods can't compete.

As a warrior, God often used forces of nature on His behalf. He parted the Red Sea, so Israel could walk through, and had it collapse back on the Egyptians. In other events of the Old Testament, God used hailstones and made the sun stand still ***(Josh. 10:1– 15).*** Other times, God empowered Israel to defeat their enemies ***(2 Sam. 5:22–25).*** God did not simply side with Israel though. When Israel was unfaithful to God, He fought against them ***(Deut. 28:25–26).***

You are not alone in your battles. When we pray to God for help, He is powerful enough to handle any situation. Jesus has already achieved victory over sin and death on the cross. He will be with us in our trials every step of the way.

DAY 23 ON THE PORCH

"*South Tuscaloosa, go to your safe place NOW!*"

This has become a familiar command from the weather dude on the moving picture box for the folks who share this piece of ground with me. My home on the southern end of Tuscaloosa, Alabama seems to be a tornado magnet.

Our safe place is about a hundred feet from our back door. When we get the orders, we head that way with everything we can carry. Valuable stuff, like my unopened Bear Bryant Coke bottles and my autographed Charlie Daniels cowboy hat. If I parted with those such things, starting over would be much worse.

But I'm glad we have a safe place. We pile in every time we have the chance. All of us... cats and dogs included. Our safe place seals shut and locks airtight like a submarine. It's buried, has ventilation and enough seating for a football squad.... smells much like one, too.

Safe place. What exactly is a *safe place*? Sometimes a safe place is not as secure. Sometimes it's shaky. Take for instance a lady I met while mom was battling dementia. I would sit and listen to her stories. She was a straight-up Charles Dickens when it came to storytelling.

"After my daughter passed, I seem to let anxiety take control of my whole life," she once told me. "The only place I would find comfort and feel safe was when my husband would hold me and let me cry until I felt better. And when he passed, I lost my safe place. We'd been married sixty years. I lost the security I'd ever known when he left."

Safe places are also used as marketing tools. They say the Toyota Camry is the safest car on the road. They back it up with a testimony of a lady who flipped her car three times and walked away. Her young daughter was in the back seat. The only fatality was a broken iPad.

Sometimes a safe place is a state of mind. I remember when my mom passed. I would find myself in my truck on some back road not even knowing how I got there. But I felt safe. It cleared my head when the country air filled my pickup cab. Pickups and backroads make you feel that way.

In 1974, Guin, Alabama had no safe place. A tornado found the town and shook it up like Kool-Aid. It was one of the most vicious tornadoes to ever hit anywhere in the U.S. The wind scales broke, so the true wind speed is still unknown. The pavement was ripped from the streets. I had family that lost everything... including their lives. Dad spent weeks helping in the area. I remember him coming home and just sitting by himself on the porch, not talking to anyone.

They said it was a generational storm. An oddity. A one-hundred-year storm. If you were alive to see this, you would never have to worry about another one like it.

"They" lied.

Thirty-seven years later— April 27, 2011. Tuscaloosa, Alabama. A hundred years came too soon. Two hundred and forty people were claimed by the tornadoes across the state. Many, right here in Tuscaloosa, including six University of Alabama Students. The city looked like a war zone.

I lost friends. I worked in search and rescue. I became part of a human chain, handing rubble to the next person, in hopes of digging out survivors. I gave out food and water. I did everything I could to help. Then I went home to my safe place .... and cried.

Over the years, I have found that safe places don't always have to *BE* safe, as long as they *FEEL* safe—a child in the arms of a mother... standing beside your wife when you're dealing with uncertainty... a backroad when your mind needs to reset.

But I have also found that nothing has ever made me feel safer than knowing that my salvation is secure because of a promise that my Savior made. I can face anything that gets thrown at me because of that promise. My safe place will withstand all other obstacles for an eternity.

If you feel like you're in a place in your life where you're always feeling worried, down and out, or just alone, then find your safe place. You can find the instructions on how to use it in John 3:16.

When there's a storm in your life... go to your Safe Place. He's waiting.

Turn your ear to me, come quickly to my rescue; be my rock of refuge, a strong fortress to save me. ~ PSALM 31:2

In this passage, David was in a challenging situation. Traps had been set for him. He was sorrowful and downcast with grief. Not only did his enemies oppose him, but he had become the object of malicious gossip. In this crisis, David describes the Lord as his refuge. God is his ultimate safe place. David knows he cannot trust in his own ability, military might, or even the strength of his fortifications. Instead, he asks God to be "my rock of refuge, a strong fortress to save me". He trusts in God's faithfulness and acknowledges that ***"my times are in your hands" (v. 15).*** He knows God ultimately wants what is best for him.

Over and over in the Psalms, God is described as a refuge. This does not mean that dangers and trials will not come our way. But during these perils, we can turn to God as ***"our refuge and strength, an ever-present help in trouble" (Ps. 46:1).***

Jesus demonstrated this trust on Good Friday. With His dying breath, He proclaimed to the Father, using the words of this psalm, ***"Into your hands I commit my spirit" (v. 5; Luke 23:46).*** God the Father was His refuge. While Jesus would endure the pain of the crucifixion, He would be vindicated in His resurrection.

Do you think of God as your refuge? He is your safe place when trials come! The psalms proclaim that God is our refuge and strength both for now and for eternity. If you can draw, try to portray a refuge, a hiding place of safety and comfort.

DAY 24 ON THE PORCH

My workshop is often neglected. I will finish my jobs, and being fatigued, I will toss my tools into the easiest place for them to land. And from this neglect, it will take me many hours to get things back to where they should be. I will spend entire days cleaning in my workshop all day. I will try to get everything back into the proper storage area. For example, I will have adjustable wrenches in four different toolbox drawers and hanging in three other places on the wall.

There are flat-head screwdrivers mixed in with Phillips-head screwdrivers. I would find metric sockets hanging out with standard sockets. Should word of this get out, *HotRod Magazine* would cancel my subscription.

But I work on it. I get everything back where it belongs. Truth be known, it shouldn't take me as long as it does. But I pause often. I relive moments in time from my childhood. After my dad went to hang out with Jesus, I acquired all his tools. He didn't have much. None of the fancy stuff. But he had everything needed to keep his Nova on the road and Momma's honey-do list at a minimum.

Every tool can tell a story. Even one of his pipe wrenches. I recalled him using this to repair lawnmowers, my bike, and as a remote control for the television antenna. He loved his tools. More so, he loved using them. He took great pride in what he could do with his tools and hands. With those two things, an assortment of cuss words, and a few cans of encouragement, he could send a man to the moon.

And he always made sure his tools were in their place. And I couldn't help but wonder if he is still like that. I am wondering if he even has tools "up there". In Heaven, do things even break? Is there a reason to even have tools? But if you enjoy such things, I would think that the Good Lord would provide us with a place to use our hands to get out of cutting grass.

Maybe Heaven doesn't work like that at all. Perhaps if something does break, a new version of it just pops into existence. I don't know. I've never been. But I've often thought about it. In fact, I probably think of Heaven more than anything else. I'm no expert on this subject. I'm no biblical theologian. I've never attended seminary vacation Bible school. I was baptized... twice. Once all the way, but still, I'm barely a full-blooded Baptist. Dad tried out the Episcopalians one time and I think I've got a touch of that in me. Two months into his experiment, he came back to the Baptist team due to engine trouble on his old Nova. Baptists believe that if Jesus turned water into wine during a wedding in Cana of Galilee, then it must be okay to have a drink changing out spark plugs.

But whoever we cheer for and whatever allegiance we pledge to tithes, I think Heaven will be the same for us all. Whatever it is. And I feel like many will be surprised by what they find. I don't know how all this works. I'm not sure what we will see when we get "there." Maybe it's just all classic cars and fishing holes. Again, I don't know, but I just don't see electric cars being allowed up there.

Perhaps they've renovated the place. Maybe the pearly gates are now titanium or streak-resistant surgical steel. You know, something easier to clean. They say they'll be mansions. But does everybody get one? Do we each get rooms in one big mansion, kind of like a frat house? Is there a maid? I'd hate to clean it. Frat boys never pick up after themselves.

Just give me a cabin next to a lake and I'll be good. Besides, mansions usually come with H.O.A. agreements. I've spent my whole life with somebody telling me what to do. When I get to Heaven, I don't want someone with a clipboard telling me when to cut my grass.

I do know that God isn't going to show us until we get there. And if we want to see it, we have to believe that it's something so amazing that it makes our eyes leak. He may not show us what's up there, but while we are down here, we can show God to the world. Kindness, compassion, and Grapicos are a good start.

Most mornings, I watch the sunrise. The first thing I think about when I think of Heaven is sunshine. Again, I don't know why. I just do. I just think that sunrises are a sneak peek at Heaven. I think Heaven's going to be a place where we won't have to worry about stuff such as the internet going out. There are no power bills, oil leaks, or fire ants. I think it'll be a place where nobody hurts nobody, and everyone's parents want them. There's so much love up there it's like watching reruns of Little House on the Prairie.

I think orphans are extinct in Heaven. I think mommas and daddies are so plentiful that they have to take turns giving kids hugs and hanging test scores and Crayola drawings on Frigidaires. I think Heaven is everything that we like here, and none of what we don't. I think it's old pickups and creek banks. Fishing poles, and dirt bikes. Dirt roads that are lined with blackberry vines.

It's Ferris wheels and go-carts. Huffy bicycles and the entire collection of G.I. Joe. It's Hotwheel cars... even the dilapidated ones... no... especially the dilapidated ones. The ones where the paint is scratched and faded, wheels warped, and dirt is built up around the axles. Those are the ones that brought the most joy. Those have to be up there.

Up there....

I imagine beautiful sounds from a baby grand piano. Angels are singing backup to The Five Blind Boys of Mississippi. People are clapping. Some even tap their toes so hard it makes you question their Baptist beliefs. Hymnals. There are tons of them. Redback editions. Most are taped together. They have that smell. You know the one. All old Baptist hymnals smell the same. It smells like a hundred years of tent revivals and window fans. Heaven will be all that. I think it will be everything that makes us smile... and nothing that prevents it... like cable news and reality TV.

I try to imagine it to be amazing, but I know I'm selling it short. I get worked up just by trying such. I can think of a million things that I think heaven is like. And still, the next time I revisit the thought, new ideas show up. In fact, I close my eyes at night to concentrate on it. I lay awake imagining the reunion. I see friends who got there before I made it. They're waiting on me. They cheer me on as I run toward them. Lynyrd Skynyrd is playing on a loudspeaker. My first dog is there. My brother and sister run to greet me.

Dale Earnhardt is there, and he has Hank Williams, Sr. on his shoulders. They're waving to me. There's a marching band. A high school one… but it's strange because they're all on key and in time.

And Daddy. I see him plain as day. He's working on his Nova. The tools I just held are somehow still with him. They are clean and laid out in order of size. They are taken care of, and not neglected. I see cane poles leaning against it. I know what this means. We are about to go fishing.

I haven't seen her yet, but I know Momma is there. She is probably leading a cooking class. I smell her peach cobbler. I know it's hers. I just know it.

I know it's amazing. I'm closing my eyes right now to tell you what I see. I see big oak trees. The kind that are easy to climb. They're huge! There are big porches with porch swings… and rocking chairs. Old men are telling stories there.

A carnival. No tickets are needed. Unlimited rides and cotton candy that don't make your hands sticky. The ride operators have all their teeth.

Golden Eagle syrup… Conecuh sausage… cat-head biscuits. It's all there. Even Blue Bell ice cream… all the flavors.

'67 Camaros… Indian motorbikes with V-twin engines. Honda three-wheelers… the real ones with red, white, and blue paint.

There are secluded fishing holes. Flat bottom boats. There's no need for those eighty-thousand-dollar bass boats in heaven. Fish practically fight over red worms there.

Some hills turn into mountains. Some valleys turn into discount flower shops. Waterfalls! Geez… there's a million of them. I've never been this close to the stars. Wow! I thought they were amazing before… but now! I'm gonna lose it if I focus on these. This is beautiful! Are you seeing this? I'm not that great at explaining things, but I hope you can imagine at least a little of it.

Man, oh man... I've never seen something so... how do I describe it?

So... beautiful! And nothing... not one thing has been neglected.

And it makes me wonder if we are neglecting the One that can get us all there.

Why is the house of God neglected? ~ NEHEMIAH 13:11

In Nehemiah 13, we read that the people of Judah had neglected the house of God. They had stopped bringing tithes to the Temple. This disobedience had a direct and negative impact on the "Levites and musicians" and the effects cascaded down to all the people of Judah. The Levites and musicians relied on Judah's tithes for their own well-being. Since the tithes were no longer being given, these workers had to leave the Temple and return to their land, so they could make a living and provide for their families.

The end result? The Temple could no longer function as it should, and worship had stopped. This might not seem like a big deal to us today, but it was a very, very big deal because the Jerusalem Temple was the only place where sacrifices could be offered to the Lord. Simply put, the worship God commanded had ceased. Dismayed at this behavior, Nehemiah once again sprang into action and set the people straight.

Following the death and resurrection of Jesus, the procedure for and positions related to worship changed. We no longer need priests and Levites to slaughter animals for sacrifice, and our worship services look a lot different. Even so, this episode in Nehemiah reminds us how important it is to honor Christ and not neglect His ministry.

DAY 25 ON THE PORCH

D o you remember the first time you ever drank homemade moonshine? Sorry, I forgot everyone didn't grow up around folks who could take sixteen original herbs and spices and turn them into a thirty-day sentence in county lockup. Let me try again.

Do you remember the first time you ever did something so stupid that it was picked up by a syndicated news network? We've all done it. We have all had these moments when as soon as you put the duct tape back up, you regret getting out of bed that day.

My dad kept a jar or six of Marion County's finest brew in his closet just for special occasions. He would bring one out when his brothers would visit from Michigan. A mason jar lid would open for family reunions. The birth of a baby. A wedding. A raise. Fresh turnip greens. New spark plugs.

And this wasn't just something he enjoyed, but he took pride in it. One of his good friends made this stuff and Dad took his job as a taste-tester seriously. He would put this stuff up against anybody's elixir. He swore it was once just water brought down in quart jars from heaven. Then one day, somebody in flip-flops, a bathrobe and hippie hair walked by and turned it into happy juice.

It was strong enough to remove rust from a Plymouth bumper. I know. It got a hold of me right around the age that I could grow pimples. I knew where Dad's stash was and helped myself to a jar. Me and a buddy rode our bikes into the woods and sampled it. We both gagged! It tasted like turpentine and bad decisions. So, we did what any self-respecting, smart young kids would do.

"I dare you to guzzle it."

"Are you kidding? No way!"

"Double-dog dare you!"

"Ah, man. Come on! Don't do this!"

"Triple-dog dare!"

There was no turning back. When the triple dog dares show up, it's serious business. Legends are made in this zone. Sissies are born. I had to choose. I did it! I swallowed enough moonshine to pickle my liver. It was horrible. I wouldn't wish this on anyone. So, I dared my buddy to chug it!

Nobody had ever mentioned that you should never partake in the whole jar. Twenty minutes later we were pushing our bikes back home to avoid peddling while intoxicated charges. We stayed sick for two whole seasons of *The Dukes of Hazzard*. It was something we would never do again.

Dad never knew. We had pulled off the perfect heist. And I believed that for years. And then, a few months before his death, he asked me if I remembered it.

"But I thought you didn't know about that?"

"I figured you boys had enough punishment. I knew my jars were safe from then on."

That's kind of how life still works for me today. I serve an almighty Father who could step in at any given minute and say, "Hey, don't do that!" But he chooses not to. And for a long time, I wondered why.

But one day it clicked. I finally figured out why God let me be so stupid. I used to wonder why he let me order *"As Seen On TV"* stuff so much. I questioned why I was allowed to grocery shop when hungry. I had questions about why I had once bought a hip-hop country CD. But one day, it hit me like an all-pro linebacker.

God can lay out our steps perfectly if He chooses, but instead, He allows us to experience the consequences of our poor choices, and the consequences of not living in His word. We have the gift of free will, and because of it, we are free to make decisions; both good and bad.

If we were to suffer no consequences for our bad choices, what motivation would there be for each of us to make good and sound decisions? More so, if God were to intervene in all our poor decisions, then we would no longer have the gift of free will; allowing the freedom to choose good and bad. Few would argue that a lesson learned with pain, struggle, and hardship is a lesson quickly forgotten.

God allows us to struggle and fail to bring humility and the realization we need Him in our lives all day, every day. Sometimes it is hard to see and understand why a loving God allows us to struggle and experience hardship, but it is because of His love for us and His desire to bring us closer to Him that He allows it. If a person lived a life filled with endless comfort and without a struggle; would they seek the Lord? I doubt many would.

As you read through this, you may realize you've made another bad decision and you've just wasted five minutes of your life. In fact, you may remember a few bad decisions you've made. You may be feeling shame, guilt, regret, or remorse. You may have done something so bad that you never have told anyone what you've done... like fishing with an expired license. Here's what I think Jesus might like to say to you today if he caught you sneaking a drink from Dad's stash:

"I don't care what bad decisions you have made. You matter to me. You are valuable to me. I love you. I will forgive you. I can restore you. I can even reverse some of the damage you have brought to your life and the lives of other people. I will welcome you back home with open arms. I died for those poor decisions that you made. They've already been paid for on the cross. Come to me and give me all the pieces of your life: the good parts, the ugly parts, the parts that embarrass you. I will take your pieces and give you my peace. Some of your past decisions have caused scars and shame. I will give you the power and wisdom to start making smart decisions that will lead to satisfaction and significance."

What a deal! Who could turn that down?

If you've realized today that you've been calling your own shots, give that control over to God. And enjoy the peace that will follow. Who knows, it may just save you from an intoxicated bike ride.

In all that has happened to us, you have remained righteous; you have acted faithfully, while we acted wickedly. ~ NEHEMIAH 9:33

Unfortunately, the Israelites did not do what the Lord required of them, and so they found themselves as "slaves in the land you gave our ancestors" *(v. 36).* They remind themselves that the Lord is a God who defends the powerless, a great comfort since they have found themselves in dire circumstances. "We are in great distress," they tell the Lord and ask Him to be who He has already shown Himself to be—"the great God, mighty and awesome, who keeps his covenant of love" *(v. 32).*

Notice that they don't elevate themselves or remind Him of their accomplishments, or even base their request on their repentance. No, they fall upon God's mercy and base their requests on His character. This, I believe, is the most important thing we can learn from today's passage. Our only hope is in God, not in our own goodness or righteousness or deservedness. When we pray, let us rest on the rock-solid foundation of who God is and never the shifting sands of who we are.

Make today's passage personal by praying that prayer for yourself. No matter what circumstance you may find yourself in, know that God is always faithful!

DAY 26 ON THE PORCH

Not long ago, I received a message from a follower: "COUSIN, I COME TO YOUR PAGE EVERY MORNING FOR YOUR STORIES! THEY ARE LIKE MY PERSONAL DEVOTIONAL!"

That was the message I woke up to. I have no idea why she was shouting this early. I haven't even had coffee yet. But I still enjoyed it. I messaged her back: THANK YOU SO MUCH, CUZ! I HOPE YOU HAVE A WONDERFUL DAY.

I almost broke my screen typing so hard, but I wasn't sure if she was hard of hearing, so I wanted her to know I appreciated her reaching out to me.

I get messages almost daily. People tell me how they are connected to my ramblings. They tell me of memories that were brought up after reading my misspelled words and bad grammar. I love every message I get. I find it enjoyable getting to know you folks. You tell me your stories, dreams, struggles, and recipes. I offer ramblings worthy of spoiled milk.

Stories are memories that explode from us. They keep things alive. They give us hope. They restore faith. And the ones I tell are no different than the ones you holler about. Our favorite singers, songwriters, comedians, preachers, or bootleggers all have one thing in common: they know how to tell a good story. And when they finish telling a story I feel connected to it–and them–in some profound way. I can relate to laughter or tears, in agreement or disagreement, but I connect powerfully with the stories they tell.

That's how it works for the rest of our lives too. We get to know each other and build friendships by sharing our stories. We are bound together by common themes, places we grew up, and taco joints that we frequent. We tell each other what we like and the things we have jointly experienced. In fact, that is how relationships and community happen... our common stories connect us and bind us together better than duct tape and fishing line.

Deep down inside, even if we can't explain it, we all yearn to be connected to a *BIGGER* story, to have our lives make a difference, and to be connected to something more. That is because our lives are all actually part of a much, much larger story. And there is *ONE* dominant story that all our stories will ultimately find their place in and finally be complete because of... God's Story.

His Story comes before, finishes, corrects, and ultimately makes sense of all other stories. Every part of our own story, and everyone else's, is actually a reflection of the Story of God. That is how God has designed things. Our life story, and all of the little pieces that make it up, actually follow the same pattern found in God's story throughout the Bible, here's what that looks like:

CREATION→FALL→REDEMPTION→RESTORATION

That's a pretty quick 4–scene version of the story found in the Bible. At times, we all screw up. Some people fall short weekly. Not me. For me, it's only daily. But our stories can help people through their hardships, shortcomings, and heartburn. To effectively share who God is, what He's up to in this world, and how he's changing our lives, we must learn how to tell our stories through the lens of this larger Story.

Unfortunately, often when a Christian tells their story (usually called "sharing our testimony") we give very little evidence to the fact that we needed to be rescued and restored by God for his glory and Kingdom purposes. And if we do mention God or Jesus in our story, we'll probably tell of some experience we had at a church service or youth camp...saying a special prayer... Then we talk about how much better our life is going today. And to tell the truth, we don't usually make ourselves look that bad, and we don't make God look all that good. We are the primary focus, the hero in our story, but we're sort of thankful for God's help along the way.

However, we can learn to tell our stories in a way that shows God is the hero of the story! and will be both salt and light to others; salty like potato chips–after getting started they'll want to hear more; and light that illuminates a path toward a new life with Jesus.

So if you've been shy in telling your faith story to others or making yourself out to be better than you really are...the next best time to make your story part of *THE* story is now.

AND IF YOU HAVE TO, HOLLER ABOUT IT!

They read from the Book of the Law of God, making it clear and giving the meaning so that the people understood what was being read. ~ NEHEMIAH 8:8

There are a few reasons this passage is a favorite of mine. First, the group listening to Scripture included ***"men and women and all who were able to understand" (v. 2).*** Scripture is for everyone! It isn't only for men, and it isn't only for adults. The assembly gathered to learn Scripture included women and children as well. That seems normal to our 21st-century minds, but it was remarkable in Nehemiah's day and time that women and children would be included along with the men—and it's a pattern Jesus continues in the New Testament.

Second, those teaching made sure the people understood Scripture. The teachers were ***"making it clear and giving the meaning so that the people understood what was being read" (v. 8).*** God wants to communicate with His people—He wants us to understand His Scripture clearly and plainly. And He has given us people to help us understand, so we can apply His Word, knowing and loving Him and others. Third, the people who gathered to learn Scripture worshiped the Lord. Learning Scripture should always provoke us to worship its Author and our Creator. This all helps us tell our stories through scripture.

God wants you to understand His Word, to worship Him, and to realize that Scripture is for all people, not just some! The Bible is for everybody. And so is your testimony. You were designed uniquely so that you could reach others. If you want to feel abundantly worthy, make sure that you are dedicated to sharing God's life-changing Word!

DAY 27 ON THE PORCH

Facebook memories are pure evil! Sure, now and then one pops up of a family trip. You're all smiling in the picture, there are chili stains on your shirt from the carnival footlong, and it makes you show off your teeth like you just got new dentures. But then, one comes up that can no longer be reproduced. It was in limited production when the original was made. And now it's as extinct as S&H Greenstamps.

I have several of those on my social media pages. Most are of my mother. One in particular, we were at the nursing home. It was a Sunday. I remember it all like it was last year's Sugar Bowl. I watched it numerous times. I was leaking salt water so much my eyes were swollen.

In the video, people are singing hymns. They are listening to scripture being read. Elderly women are clapping. Elderly men are snoring. One lady is asking whose birthday it is. It's great! These folks are ancient, but gosh I loved visiting with them. They looked at me as if I was still a kid. I looked at them as if they were treasures.

I'm so glad to have captured moments like these. I can remember how much they enjoyed it. They are all forgetting aches and pains. A man plays the piano. He would quickly tell you he's a song leader. He was accused of being a minister of music once. It still leaves a bad taste in his mouth.

"That sounds too official," he would say. "When you sing from Baptist hymnals as old as these, song leader is as fancy as it needs to be."

He sits at the upright in the cafeteria and plays the classics. "Old Rugged Cross" is a fan favorite. "When The Roll Is Called Up Yonder" is another knee slapper. He knows all the good ones.

Wheelchairs roll in by the dozen. Everyone smiles. Some have forgotten their dentures. They have their favorite buddies to sit by. They park in rows. Early birds get seats up front. Stragglers sit in the nosebleeds. The more the song leader plays, the more people's hips wake up. Three songs in, half of the tenants are tapping their toes like full-blooded Pentecostals.

He sings "I Saw the Light," "Blessed Assurance", and "I Surrender All." After each, the residents of the nursing home clap. Some are louder than others. Some are woken up by the commotion. After the song singing, hand clapping, and church service are done, the real fun begins. This is the part I always enjoyed.

I get to talk to most of them. They like it when I visit. Likewise, I smile the entire time. A few would gather around Momma. I would ask how their day was going. I would always hear about arthritis, sugar pills, and roommates that snore.

They tell me stories about gardening, the first time they saw a television, and they remembered when Elvis was invented. I'd listen like I would be tested later. It's history to me. Good history. It's a time as old as tomato plants.

"I was a tugboat captain once," one old man tells me. "I went all up and down Alabama's rivers. Did I ever tell you 'bout that?"

Every Sunday he told me about that.

"No sir," I'd say. "I'd love to hear about it."

"About what?"

Some would start to leave, while others lingered. They all had stories to share. They just didn't have enough listeners that had signed up. One of Mom's Bingo buddies holds Momma's hand. She sits and smiles, never saying anything. Another lady zooms by us, sending dining chairs flying. She is still figuring out her new electric wheels.

"Slow down, Edna," a nurse hollers. "You're going to break something... again."

It's almost lunchtime. The cafeteria comes alive with smells of canned vegetables, baked chicken, and artificial fiber. I sit with Mom and her friends. Mom is having a good day. It's almost enough to make me think we may make a turn for the better. Almost.

We talk over bowls of instant banana pudding. I could never bring myself to tell her that this was powder just a few minutes ago.

There's chatter all around us. Out of the blue, one of Momma's friends tells me she used to be a teacher. That's how most of these conversations start. Something pops into their memories, and we all get to experience it.

"I was a librarian," she added.

"I'm a Baptist," another lady tells her. "But we are all the same in Jesus' eyes."

I hear the keys on the piano getting pounded. A nurse heads that way.

"I used to play," a little lady explains. "Give me just a minute to get my hands working right."

She tried again. It's better. I start recognizing some of the notes. Others do, too. A little old man takes a break from his sweet potato. He starts singing. "Twas grace that taught my heart to fear."

Mom's friend joins in, "And grace my fears relieved."

Then another... and another. Mom picks up a line. She's smiling as she sings. "How precious did that grace appear, the hour I first believed."

I noticed a nurse mouthing the words. A server is humming. Before long the whole cafeteria is hollering the words to "Amazing Grace." Nobody is on key. They're all a word or two off from where they need to be. And it's the most beautiful thing I've ever seen. Before I know it, I'm hollering like Alan Jackson.

Everyone claps when the music finishes.

"I don't remember any other ones," the pianist informs us.

"That's okay, sweetie. You did great," a nurse tells her.

"Can I play it again," she asks.

"Play all you want."

She struck up again. Everyone sang again. Momma found her voice on this round. She's singing as if Jesus is directing her. I didn't know it then, but this was the last service that Mom would attend. We only had a few more trips to the cafeteria. A few short weeks later, she got to sing to Jesus face-to-face.

I'm glad we experienced that day. It's a memory that I needed this morning. And when it came up, it stung like a hornet. But the more I recalled that day, the more I smiled.

As I wheeled Momma back to her room that day, she told me that she had fun.

"This was one of the best days I've had in a while," she told me.

"Yes, Momma. It was one of mine, too."

In a room full of fiber pills and liver spots, the world was a better place that day. Men and women from all walks of life, worshipping God the only way they know how. And that way is beautiful.

Isn't it a great concept when we look at each and know we are different, but still all created in the image of God? And when we grow old, we all carry some of our life's lessons along the journey and bless others with them. We are all the same, but just doing different things. Isn't it great that God created us that way?

There are different kinds of service, but the same Lord. ~ 1 CORINTHIANS 12:5

Nehemiah shared God's work, encouraged the people, and rejected the scorn of naysayers. But it was God's people who got to work rebuilding Jerusalem's walls. The chapter may seem a bit boring—it simply lists people and the sections of the wall they rebuilt. It's kind of like the list of acknowledgments at the back of a book, except that it comes right at the front. But if you take the time to read through the people and the work they did, it's absolutely fascinating. Everyone went to work including goldsmiths, priests, and Levites— people who relied on a wide variety of work to support their families pitched in to rebuild the broken-down wall, towers, and gates surrounding Jerusalem. What could have been a huge almost unsurmountable task, became possible when so many contributed. This was an equalizing team effort if there ever was one!

However, verse 5 singles out a group who refused to help: The "nobles (from Tekoa) would not put their shoulders to the work under their supervisors." They didn't want to work for a boss other than themselves. They viewed themselves as too important, too powerful, and too big to humble themselves and join the rest of God's people in rebuilding Jerusalem.

As Christians, we must resist the temptation to think of ourselves as "better than others." Instead, we should remember that we are all part of one body, and no part is more important than another. What can you do today to develop humility and a heart to serve the Lord in any capacity?

DAY 28 ON THE PORCH

At one time, I had almost forgotten what it was like to dream. I am not talking about dreaming of swimming in oceans or having coupons for all-you-can-eat buffets. I mean bigger things. Career moves. What I wanted to do in life. Those types of things. But I had to grow up. That was the kid inside me. Childish dreams. Big dreams only come true in the movies.

All I had ever known was a life that worked my mom and dad to skin and pork rinds. We didn't have much to offer the world, but I still dreamed. I would lie awake at night and think of all the places in the world that I'd like to go to. I would think of being someone that made a difference. My name would be one that created smiles on faces. And I stored all those big dreams in places that only I could get to, for fear of being laughed at.

One such dream was writing. It was my escape to a world I could only dream of. We could barely afford 3-in-1 oil for my bike chain, but when I wrote, I was a million miles away and worth more than Willie Nelson's illegal garden. I would write about faraway places and exploring jungles, caves, and Super Walmarts.

I would pretend to be writing for a newspaper or a magazine. I fell short of hoping to write a book because that was too big to dream about. Having my name on a book that was sold in stores was too farfetched for someone like me. But still, I pretended, and I dreamed.

My sister had a small portable typewriter. It was light blue and came with a top that made it into what looked like a suitcase. When she wasn't home, I would sit in her room, and pretend to write. It was horrible. Punctuation was in the wrong place. Words were misspelled. I would routinely use past and present tense in the same sentence describing the same event. Much the same way I write today. But now, I've improved. Now, I spell much better... thanks to autocorrect. Which also has saved my Baptist membership. I can't even spell a cuss word if I try. For example, I am trying to tell you right now that I feel as tired as an ununionized coal miner who has worked his ash off. See! It just won't happen.

But those dreams died. I gave up hope, and I went to work right out of school in the first place which would give me a shot. Sure, I had a few college courses that I survived, but I started building mobile homes to pay bills. I was cutting grass on the side. I learned to weld. I built farm equipment. I did factory work. I did a lot of things in exchange for my dreams. And all of those things I am thankful for. They instilled a work ethic in me, much like my old man. They taught me a lot about life. They developed trade skills in me that save me a ton of money now, repairing my own junk.

Decades later I started dreaming again. I traded a typewriter for a laptop. New-age writing takes new-age technology. Now, I can use bad grammar and made-up words without ever having to change the ink ribbon. And once I figured out that there was still hope for the kid inside of all of us, it changed everything.

I'll never forget it. I was in a big chain store the first time I saw it. A book. It had my name on it. I squealed like Taylor Swift. I picked it up. I was holding a book which read "by Russell L. Estes". And that's a moment I will never forget. I did a happy dance. I was right there in the new release section shaking my moneymaker as if auditioning for the Rockettes. And then I lost it. Tears showed up before I could stop them. My emotions hit me like everything in my life had just come rushing back. All the dreams. All the heartaches. The refusals. The letdowns.

But in my hands, I was holding the proof that it is okay to keep dreaming. And what I felt is what everyone wants to feel—important. Not just to other important people, but to myself. I felt like that even a poor kid with nary a credential worth mentioning may have a chance. That's all anyone wants. A chance. People have been wanting that since Jesus was turning water into Grapico.

I was in a rough spot. My mother had just passed – the last of my core group. My father had gone ahead of her many years ago. So had my sister. Then my brother. I was the last of "us". I felt like my path was unpaved. I felt like it led to nowhere. But then again, unpaved roads in the middle of nowhere have always been my favorite places. So that's what I started writing about.

In a way, writing saved me. Not in a life-or-death type of way, but something almost as important. A way that gave me a purpose again. A way for me to make a difference. And even though the idea of me being a writer makes about as much sense as me being a brain surgeon, somehow, I dreamed again. And it happened.

Which means some kid out there might be working his hindquarters off, while his or her dream takes a backseat. And if you're that kid, whether you are eight or eighty, I want you to know that your dream isn't dead. Neither is the kid in you who is still dreaming.

I hope you at least think about it. Like really, really think that, "Hey, I may have a shot at this." And if all you do on day one of realizing it's doable, is writing it down, then your one step closer.

And if you write down your dream, don't hide it where you only know where it is. Tape it to the mirror. Every time you look at yourself, you'll see your dream. And you'll realize that your dream is still there... inside you... ready to explode out.

I hope you go for it. I hope you chase your dream like a coon hound after a hyped-up possum on meth.

I hope one day, you do a happy dance in the middle of a crowded big-box store. I hope people congratulate you. And I hope you realize that you are important. And you find out that you were the entire time.

But more than that... more than anything else in this whole wide world, I hope a kid is reading this that is on the verge of giving up. I hope they realize that if somebody as simple and unimportant as me can be happy about dreaming, you can too. And I hope that kid decides not to give up.

Giving up is the only thing that kills dreams. And I know that deep inside of you, that dream is still glowing. It may be just an ember, with hardly any fire left in it, but given the chance, it will come back to life into a raging inferno.

And I hope that the kid in you does too. I hope the kid inside of you makes a comeback so big that Netflix wants to document it. Perhaps that kid feels like a complete screw-up. Maybe they've been told they will never amount to a hill of beans. But I want you to know those people that say that are wrong. They couldn't be more wrong if they tried to suggest that peanuts don't belong in Coke.

But it's up to you to take that first step. Perhaps you have everything planned out, knowing God was with you, and all that was left was to begin— returning to school, starting foster care classes, or sharing the gospel with that one person in your life. The beginning takes courage!

Come, let us rebuild the wall of Jerusalem, and we will no longer be in disgrace. ~ NEHEMIAH 2:17

And courage is exactly what we see in Nehemiah and the rest of the people of Jerusalem who would rally with him to rebuild the city's walls. Once Nehemiah finished his reconnaissance mission to learn the lay of the land, he saw just in what a bad shape the city had been. Nehemiah gathered the rest of the people of Jerusalem and shared his vision with them.

Most importantly, Nehemiah told them all God had already done for him, ensuring that this was not some hair-brained idea from a Persian official: ***"I also told them about the gracious hand of my God on me and what the king had said to me" (v. 18)***. Nehemiah's testimony of God's favor gave the people of Jerusalem the courage they needed to begin the enormous task: ***"They replied, 'Let us start rebuilding.' So they began this good work" (v. 18)***.

Sometimes in our lives, we will be like Nehemiah, called by God to lead for Him in a certain area, perhaps in our family or at our job. Other times we will be like the rest of the people in Jerusalem, called by God to follow someone as they lead out in a way God has called them to. At all times God calls us to trust in Him and go courageously wherever He leads.

Is there something in your life that God has called you to do, but you've been too afraid to begin? Like Nehemiah, share your plans with those who can help you, trust the Lord, and get to work.

DAY 29 ON THE PORCH

I love the mornings when I am at home. I can sit on my patio and listen to the world come alive. It's peaceful. The only sound is the birds, the wind through the leaves, and the Waste Management garbage truck making its rounds.

I just finished reading my Bible and devotional. I am expecting God to holler at me about what He wants me to take from today's lesson.

Nothing...

I pray to Him. I ask for guidance on how I can do His work today. Zilch...

I don't know what I've done. I often get the silent treatment from my wife, but I usually know what caused it. I have a long history of doing and saying stupid stuff. Her, being the Proverbs thirty-one woman she is, chooses the nursery rhyme "If You Can't Say Anything Nice, Don't Call Your Husband A Moron."

I've gotten the silent treatment more times than a public library. I would much rather hash it out. I'm not good at silence. I've hollered, squealed, and caused a ruckus most of my life. Silence makes me nervous. But this morning, I am accepting the silence because I've been here before in God's silence. I know where this leads.

Have you ever felt as if God was giving you the silent treatment?

Perhaps you are going through a physical illness, and despite your prayers for healing, the Lord has not intervened. You've reminded Him of your contributions and commitments. You even show Him the receipt where you donated to the Baptist Potluck and Buck Dance Festival. Your contribution helped the youth department take a trip to the gospel revival at Dave and Busters.

Maybe you're fervently seeking His direction for a major decision, and He's just not answering. You've called so much that you are starting to think He blocked you and reported you to Mark Elliot Zuckerberg.

At such times, questions run through our minds: Is He listening? Does He even care? Why won't He help me? Is His phone going through an update?

If you've experienced a situation like this, you are not alone. Remember Lazarus? You know his story. But what about his sisters who prayed for him? Have you ever thought about how they felt? Mary and Martha knew the heartache, confusion, and disappointment of having their hopes dashed. They got plum mad because Jesus wouldn't respond to their social media messages.

When their brother Lazarus became sick, they sent a text to Jesus. But when He got the message, He waited two more days before starting His journey *(John 11:1-7).* Maybe He was doing yard work. After all, during the time of year this occurred, the petunias were blooming. Perhaps He was in the middle of an *Andy Griffith Show* marathon. You just can't get up and go heal somebody in one of those. Perhaps He was just tired and needed two days off, which is what led to the invention of the weekend.

Mary and Martha expected the Lord to drop everything to come and heal their brother. They were nervous. They had no idea why Jesus wouldn't at least call them back. Can you imagine their anxiety and perplexity as they waited and watched Lazarus's condition worsen— until one day he died?

"Where was Jesus? Why hadn't He come?" They wondered.

I can sympathize with Mary and Martha because I've also experienced God's silence. Not like this morning, but on much more important things. Most recently, it was while going through my cancer battle. I was asking the Lord to show me His will concerning a situation that would significantly affect my future. I felt a strong calling to use cancer for God's glory, but how can you even do that?

Night after night, I faithfully prayed and read the Scriptures. Still, no answer came. One night, in desperation, I walked out into my backyard. I stood and looked up at the gazillion stars. Most of my prayers are silent. God still heard them. But this time, I verbally prayed —shouted even.

It wasn't a flash of lighting moment where everything became clear, but I started realizing how I could glorify Him as I climbed my mountain. And eventually, in His perfect time, God gave me unmistakably clear guidance.

Silent times are often God's means of preparation for something greater. Think about the story of Lazarus. The Lord delayed for good reason: instead of healing an illness, He was planning to raise His friend to life. In that way, He accomplished His Father's will and brought Him glory. That incident convinced many of the Jews that Jesus was their Messiah.

God's silence is never random or indifferent. Every time He's quiet, He has a good reason. It could be that . . . we're not ready to listen. Sometimes the problem is not God's silence, but our inability to hear. If we're so caught up in this world and all its incentives, our ears won't be tuned for His voice. He could be shouting, and we still wouldn't hear Him.

At other times, we think we know more than He does. We think we have our own remedy for our problem. We know what *WE* want, and we hope that His answer is the same. When it's not, we tend to say, "Okay, that wasn't God." So, we wait... and wait... and wait, because the answer He sent didn't fit our wants.

God's silence is not forever. In His perfect time, the answer will come. And if you faithfully and patiently wait for Him, you'll discover that your relationship with Him has deepened through the experience. You will have learned to sit with Him through silence, not relying on His activity to encourage you, but simply delighting in His presence. If you make this a habit in your life, fretting and fuming will disappear, and in their place, you'll find the most satisfying relationship possible.

You'll be able to sit on your porch and smile. The birds will sing their songs. The garbage truck will play its tune. And you'll be able to have peace knowing God is already directing you.

My people would not listen to me; Israel would not submit to me. ~ PSALM 81:11

Tragically, this is how the Israelites in this scripture mocked the prophet Isaiah and his word from the Lord. Possibly drunk, they said the prophet's words sounded like nonsense. To whom did the prophet think he was speaking? Babies? The line translated "a rule for this, a rule for that" is probably, according to the NIV footnote, "meaningless sounds mimicking the prophet's words." Another source compares it to childish babbling or baby talk, thus connecting it to verse 9.

Since the people of Israel wouldn't listen, scorning the prophet's warning as meaningless, God would speak to them in a foreign language, words they wouldn't understand *(v. 11)*. This is a reference to the coming Assyrian conquest. God had once said to Israel, ***"This is the resting place, let the weary rest" and "This is the place of repose"*** *(v. 12)*. This reference evokes the nation's past failure. At the border of Canaan, they had refused to trust God. Both at that time and in Isaiah's day, God intended blessings for His people, but instead, Israel incurred His judgment because of their disobedience.

The word of the Lord would mock them in the same way they'd mocked Him. The result? They would fall. "They will be injured and snared and captured." Pridefully, they thought their status as the "people of God" protected them, but they didn't listen to God—a failure on their part. God had told them many times the consequences of their covenant unfaithfulness.

When confronted with the truth of God's Word, what is your attitude? No, really. How do you feel about it? Troubled? Guilty? Indifferent? Is the silence you hear because you've blocked out God's answer because it wasn't what you wanted to hear? Perhaps it's time to turn up our hearing aids.

<hr>

DAY 30 ON THE PORCH

<hr>

I can tell when I rush my time with God. It can throw off my entire day. I start each day by reading His Word and spending prayer time with Him. I can get my mind right for the whole day with devotion and prayer. And the mornings are perfect for this because I am the only early riser in the house. Everyone is still sleeping when me and God have our talk. Not that I don't enjoy mornings with my family, but when they're up, as a father and husband, I feel they should have my attention.

But when I'm by myself... game on! Just me, my Savior, and my coffee.... one on one with Jesus. And it makes me wonder what it was like when Jesus walked the earth and prayed to His Father. I do know He arose early to pray. It's right there in the Good Book.

"Very early in the morning, while it was still dark, Jesus got up, left the house, and went off to a solitary place, where he prayed." ~ Mark 1:35

I've always been indescribably drawn to the private life of Jesus. All the teachings and miracles are well known, but what did Jesus do when others weren't around? When others weren't watching, how did he act? When it was just Him and His Father, what was it like? That's what makes a relationship personal and true.

The moments that interest me most are when Jesus withdrew to quiet places to pray, each prayer time a compelling picture of the Son's intimate connection with His Father. I can find some of the answers in the Book of Mark, which tells us that while it was still dark, Jesus slipped out of the house and went to a secluded place to meet with His Father. Mark doesn't tell us what morning this was. But we do know this prayer time followed a full day of healing the sick and casting out demons. After that kind of day, you would think Jesus might have slept in ... just for an hour or two. I probably would have, or at least wanted to. But not Jesus. He awakened before the sun peeked over the horizon to be refreshed and renewed for the ministry awaiting Him that day.

Oh, how I would love to know what Jesus said. How long did He pray? What did He pray? Could He audibly hear His Father's response? Were the angels with Him? And more practically, did His mind wander? Mine does. Sometimes I find myself praying and my mind travels to my "to-do" list. Or I begin praising God but then the concerns weighing on my heart push through and usher out my praise.

I imagine Jesus' mind didn't wander because He knew in those solitary places He was sitting in the very presence of His Father. And what I forget, perhaps many of us do, is that when we pray, we too sit in the very presence of God, our Father. Although our eyes cannot visibly see Him, I picture Him drawing near, bending close to hear our every word. His Spirit surrounds us. His hands lift our faces heavenward. His ears fixed on every cry of our hearts ... the praises, the confessions, the anxieties, the fears, the doubts... He hears them all.

Sometimes it's hard to wake up early. Hard to focus. And most of all, it's hard to fathom that the God of the universe, who holds the entire world in His hands, has time to hear our little prayers. But not only does He have the time, He calls us to come to Him. *Jeremiah 33:3* says, *"Call to me and I will answer you and tell you great and unsearchable things you do not know"*.

I desire to pray like Jesus, knowing wholeheartedly that I'm one-on-one with Christ. On the days that I find this free-minded solitude... those days go so much better.

Blessed are those who fear the LORD, who find great delight in his commands. ~ PSALM 112:1

God's Word can do the same for you. Psalms 111 and 112 are a matched pair. They both follow an acrostic pattern. The first focuses on God; the second focuses on godly people, that is, people who "fear the Lord." Godly people "find great delight in his commands". In other words, the Word of God instructs and empowers them in the way of godliness. This way includes righteousness or uprightness grace and compassion, generosity and justice, and steadfast faith. There is a particular emphasis on generosity to the poor *(v. 4).* Having received blessings, we want to bless others.

As we walk in God's way, we're richly blessed, for example, with children. The Lord might also bless us with material wealth. Good things seem to happen for God's people even in bad times. They stand firm in their convictions and are remembered with honor after they're gone. They're not anxious when bad news or dark times come. Instead, their faith in the Lord removes fear, makes them spiritually secure, and gives them victory over their enemies. The psalm doesn't say our life will be all sunshine and roses, but rather that, because the fear of the Lord is the center of the godly person's life, He will bless them with Himself.

Find time to talk to Jesus. You'll be surprised at how much better your day will be.

DAY 31 ON THE PORCH

He said, "Come ahead." Jumping out of the boat, Peter walked on the water to Jesus. But when he looked down at the waves churning beneath his feet, he lost his nerve and started to sink. He cried, "Master, save me!" Jesus didn't hesitate. He reached down and grabbed his hand. Then he said, "Faint-heart, what got into you?" ~ Matthew 14:29-30-31

I rarely start any of my ramblings with a scripture. I have most often found that it flows better to tell a brief story and throw in a scripture or two. That way, the non-believers and the few that don't pledge their allegiance to the Crimson Tide are tricked into getting some "God learning".

But today is different. I feel as if this one needs to come out swinging. One, because for many years, I had no clue when Jesus was calling me to do anything. I was afraid to take any first steps. I couldn't tell you the difference between Jesus guiding my steps, and the pains from the tacos I had hours earlier. And when I did feel like it was Jesus, I would hesitate.

And that leads us to the million-dollar question of the day: **Do you have faith to follow your calling?** When God lays something on your heart, are you afraid to step outside your comfort zone?

Peter wanted to experience what Jesus was experiencing and wanted it so bad that he stepped out. He started walking on the water. Something that is totally impossible in the natural world. He had faith that Jesus would save him from drowning.

There may be something that you want to do, that in your eyes, seems impossible. You might want to start a business. You may want to go back to school; but now you're married with children and working, so you're wondering where you will find the time.

Sometimes there can seem to be too many obstacles standing between you and your dream. Sometimes those obstacles look like insurmountable mountains. But I have good news for you: there is nothing too big for God!

The Bible says that all things are possible to those who believe. Can you believe God will find a way to pay for school? Can you believe God will show you everything you need to do to get that business started? Well like Jesus said, "Be it unto you according to your faith". Some translations read, "Become what you believe".

When Jesus told Peter, "Come", Peter believed in the words of Jesus, and he started doing the impossible. We must do the same thing. We must meditate on the Word of God and think on the Word of God until we know that we can become what we believe. Peter was doing fine until he took his eyes off Jesus and began looking at the waves and turning his attention to how hard the wind was blowing. It was only then that he began to sink.

We must take our eyes off circumstances and keep our focus on the Mountain Mover. Yes, the circumstances are real. Yes, we must count the cost before we step out. But we must remember that once we know that we are in the will of God, and God is telling us to step out, we must be like Moses when he was facing the Red Sea. Pharaoh and his army were behind him, and the Red Sea was in front of him. God didn't tell him, "I'm sorry man. I wasn't prepared for the Red Sea. I guess you're stuck". No. God told him to stretch out that rod and move forward. When Moses did, God parted the Red Sea and the Israelites walked on dry land. It would have been okay if the Israelites walked on muddy ground, but the Bible says the Israelites walked on dry ground!

When God tells us to move, we must trust that He will go before us and make the crooked places straight. Remember Jesus told Peter to come out on the water. We must step out when Jesus tells us to. We must move when we are prompted in our spirits and when we know that we are in God's timing.

God has great plans for us. He wants us to step out of the boat that we are currently in; but when we do, we must make sure He has called us out of the boat, and we must make sure we are prepared for what is outside our boat. When we are, and we start walking, get ready! You are about to do the impossible!

What does it mean to answer Jesus' call? At its simplest explanation, Christ's call was 'Follow me.' He asked men and women for their personal allegiance. He invited them to learn from him, to obey his words, and to identify themselves with his cause. To follow Christ is to renounce all lesser loyalties.

"Come, follow me," Jesus said, "and I will send you out to fish for people." ~ MATTHEW 4:19

In Matthew 4, Jesus' public ministry had begun. John the Baptist had been taken into custody, and, because of the growing threat, Jesus left Nazareth and settled in Capernaum. There He preached publicly a message of repentance, an acknowledgment of sin, and a turning from it *(v. 17).*

Two fishermen, Peter and Andrew *(v. 18),* were familiar with Jesus since Andrew had been a disciple of John the Baptist. They'd already considered Jesus' mission and message. When Jesus said to them, "Come, follow me" *(v. 19),* they were prepared to immediately leave their boats, their occupation, and their livelihood—and follow Jesus.

Next, Jesus called another pair of brothers, James, and John, who were fishing with their father. When He called them, "immediately they left the boat and their father and followed him" *(v. 22).* The magnitude of their obedience is highlighted by the fact that they also left their family.

While discipleship was a common concept in the Jewish culture, being a disciple of Jesus was distinct. The traditional model involved a rabbi, demonstrating his teaching of the Torah, and his disciples following his pattern. Certainly, Jesus' disciples were committed to His teaching, but they were even more committed to His person. Jesus was not only offering them temporal teacher training but also inviting them into an eternal kingdom relationship.

The call of first disciples highlights Jesus' authority. When He calls us to follow, the only appropriate response is obedience and utter dedication. A renouncing of all "lesser loyalties." A complete realignment of focus and life.

DAY 32 ON THE PORCH

Life can throw curveballs at you with no warning. Everything will be cruising along just fine, then a brick wall comes out of nowhere, and you find yourself in a rut. Not just a rut, but more like a trench. A ditch even—one so deep you can't get out even with four-wheel-drive and a camouflage ballcap. There's been days when I was so deep, at any minute I may have discovered the lost tomb of Alexander the Great.

And here's the kicker—I don't know why. It's not the cancer. It's not the treatments. It's not the days I feel like a flat possum. I'm not good at explaining these things but if I were to give it a shot, it would go something like this: I feel like I could be doing more with this season in my life… and I'm not. I feel like I've lost my **purpose.**

I was drowning in self-pity one Sunday when I was hit square in the face by a sermon prepared just for me… at least I felt that way. I was at my home church, Valley View Baptist in Tuscaloosa, Alabama, and our pastor, Brother Billy Joy was bringing the heat! That man was hollering God's Word like was in a rap battle. That rascal can flat-out spew a sermon straight from Mount Sinai.

"And we know that all things work together for good to them that love God, to them who are the called according to his purpose," he shouted at me as he caught his breath between hollering campaigns.

Purpose. There's that word again.

Here I am... worried about *my* purpose... when all along I should be worried about *HIS* purpose. God is working in the favor of those who love Him. Well, I love Him. I should be in a good place, right? But here's the statement that got me. This one right here made me take deep breaths. When Brother Billy hauled off and slung this one, it nailed me...

"God isn't interested in changing your circumstances, but changing who you are."

Wow! It's not about what I'm going through. It's about what I can do to glorify Him through it. It's about making me more aware of what He already does for me, and how I respond to that.

All of a sudden, I am climbing out of that rut. I don't even care about Alexander the Great anymore. I am thankful. For everything! Even the stuff that I didn't think about being thankful for before.

Things like saturated fat. Thick-cut bacon, cured hams, and fried bologna. Memories of sheets and clothes that just came off a summer clothesline. Momma stands right in the middle of those memories. Old TV shows, like The Lone Ranger, Cisco Kid, and Lassie. As a boy, I could dial in the UHF knob to play reruns of *Andy Griffith, Little Orphan Annie, Hee Haw*, and the *Grand Ole Opry*. I lived for these shows. I'm thankful for them.

I'm thankful for a lot more. Hear me out— like tomatoes. Tomatoes remind me of so much more than sandwiches. They remind me of a man who grew them outside, under his bedroom window. A man who taught me that raising tomatoes was a passage of men, and we are to be proud of them and talk about them in the workplace. It's biblical that we share garden tomatoes with coworkers. That man was my dad.

Momma. The woman who meant the world to me. "Thankful" is not a strong enough word for her. Even when the world came crashing down, she taught me three words that changed everything... "I love you." And then she taught me three more words that she knew I would one day need more than ever — "Trust God's Plan." I'm thankful for those lessons.

I am thankful for every word *Lewis Grizzard* ever wrote. That sapsucker could straight up make the phone book look like poetry. My whole life, all I ever wanted to be was a writer of books. I finally was able to find someone gullible enough to publish my ramblings. I feel like I'm dreaming when I see my book in a store. I still don't consider myself a writer. A bad storyteller, maybe... but a writer?

Biscuits. Grits. Family reunions. Old cars. Older pickups. Deer... better yet, deer dogs. Fishing when I should be working. Sleeping when I should be fishing. I'm thankful for those in rapid fire.

Oddly enough, I'm thankful for the people who hurt me—they know who they are. They were the ones that let me down more often than a McDonald's ice cream machine. Funny. I thought they were friends. They weren't... unless, of course, I was still within earshot of their words. I'm thankful for those people because I learned valuable lessons from them... and I'm thankful for their words they didn't know would make it back to me. Their words pushed me harder to find my purpose.

Words. I'm thankful for words. I use them to express myself. Like this total mess you're reading. But also, I'm thankful for the words that made it back to me. They helped me realize the aforementioned thought above.

I'm thankful for you— the ones still punishing yourself by reading this far. I don't know where all of you are. I don't know if your life is good or bad. Some of you may be in your own rut right now. I hope you're not. But I don't know.

I don't know if you sleep in your Pontiac or a three-story mansion. I don't know if you've ever been anywhere farther than work and the Piggly Wiggly. But I am thankful for you. I want you to know that most of the time when I write these God-awful things, I'm thinking about you. And sometimes, I write them because I need to read them worse than you do. I never knew I could be a writer. I still don't believe it.

But since I care about you, I want you to know that you can be whatever you decide to be. Even if bad things get in the way. Bad things don't last forever.

And I want you to know that not too long ago, I was in a rut... maybe a trench. All because I thought I didn't know if I was using this cancer as God intended. It can be a powerful testimony if it's about God, and not me.

Not long ago, I thought my purpose was something else. But one Sunday, a good man told me that if I counted my blessings, I would be in a good spot. He reminded me that all things, not some things, but all things would work together for good things, for those that love God. He said that God is already working in my favor, and for those who are called according to his **purpose**, He has our back.

Man, I love God! I found my purpose... He is my purpose.

Now go; I will help you speak and will teach you what to say. ~ EXODUS 4:12

But there are times when God uses those things, we aren't good at, for His purpose. In Exodus we see that happen to Moses. When God called Moses to bring His people out of Egypt, Moses objected several times. His first objection was his own inadequacy: "Who am I...?". To which God responded, ***"I will be with you" (v. 12).*** God promised His presence and a future hope. He painted a picture for Moses of the redeemed Israelites worshiping on that same mountain.

Moses was not convinced. He responded with a second, odd objection. He didn't know how to identify God. The Lord responded, ***"I AM WHO I AM" (v. 14)***—a rich name, affirming God's eternal self-existence. God instructed Moses how to explain His identity and assured him that the Israelites would listen.

Moses still faltered, claiming his own lack of credibility. The Israelites wouldn't believe him. So, God, then, performed three signs through Moses, demonstrating the power with which Moses would be authorized to act.

Even these miracles did not embolden Moses, and he responded with one final concern—his own lack of eloquence. God reminded Moses that He made his mouth, and He would provide the words. At which point, Moses finally whined: ***"Please send someone else" (v. 13).*** And God got angry.

God may call you outside of your comfort zone to do something that seems beyond your ability. That's the point! God promises His presence and His power because ultimately it is His work, not ours. I was once afraid to write books and share my thoughts with the world. I was afraid to speak in front of crowds. But now, I do both. Not because I became better at either... but because God equipped me and gave me a purpose—a purpose to glorify Him through me.

DAY 33 ON THE PORCH

I wait for it every morning. I don't want to miss a single one. I absolutely love the sunrise. I love to see the sun peeking through the trees. But what if I have seven thousand sunrises left in me? And... what if I only have one?

We do not know how long we have to live, so we should live every day with gusto. We should enjoy every day as if it were our last. There are hundreds of things that can make us feel alive, full of joy, just as the sunrise does to me: A baby's laughter. A walk with the love of your life. Hanging out with friends. A good book. Banana pudding, the good kind, with meringue on top. Fried bologna, thick slice. A '69 Camaro. There are many things and ways that we can enjoy life.

With so many opportunities at every turn, it's alarming to realize that one in ten Americans experience depression at some point in their lives. I've caught cases of it myself. I've been temporarily drawn into its lair during dark times in my life. Death of a loved one... lifesaving surgery of my son... cancer diagnosis... there have been many things that stole my sunrise.

Why is that? More often than not it's because we've let our circumstances dictate our enjoyment of life. When circumstances are calm and favorable, we more easily enjoy the simple things in life. When they are chaotic, we let even the little things stress us out and the enjoyment of life seems like a fleeting memory.

So, what's the secret? It's our perspective. When we keep our focus on the promises found in God's Word and on His love for us, our big and scary circumstances seem much smaller and are more easily dealt with, leaving more time to enjoy life. (God Is Bigger)

That's what God really wants for us: to enjoy life. It's through our enjoyment of life and the joy we carry about us that attracts others to Him. If we are down in the dumps all the time, we don't make a relationship with God look attractive.

In His final prayer, Jesus prayed that His disciples would experience the full measure of his joy—now. He didn't pray for joy only during the good times. He prayed for us to have His joy in the middle of rush-hour traffic, screaming kids, and a darkening world. He doesn't want us to wait for heaven to be full of joy.

Jesus' joy has a divine purpose: to reveal Him. He desires to fill us with overflowing joy, to proclaim His victory to the world over life's worst conditions—even in the face of hurricanes, plagues, terrorism, and especially in a battle for our life.

Joy flows from a foundation of truth. So many times, we focus on imaginary troubles. We cloud our minds with issues that we are not even dealing with. But Jesus reminds us that joy comes from knowing the Father through the Son.

As you reflect on your life, whether you're 18, 28, 38, 48, or 88, choose to live in the fullness of joy by taking the time to smile more ... and by living each moment fully aware of God's love for you. Choose to go out today with a purpose to be happy, have a great attitude, and enjoy the day. You'll be glad you did.

So, I commend the enjoyment of life, because there is nothing better for a person under the sun than to eat and drink and be glad. Then joy will accompany them in their toil all the days of the life God has given them under the sun. ~ Ecclesiastes 8:15

This day is holy to our Lord. Do not grieve, for the joy of the LORD is your strength. ~ NEHEMIAH 8:10

Ezra and his associates had just finished helping the people of God understand Scripture. The people, understandably, ***"had been*** *weeping as they listened to the words of the Law" (v. 9)*. They had likely realized all the ways in which they had failed to obey the Lord, and the Spirit was convicting them of sin. That is a good and right response, and I only wish that we would all more fully recognize our sin and respond with weeping at the Spirit's conviction.

However, Nehemiah quickly tells the people that this was not the day for weeping and mourning. It was more like a wedding reception, a time of *"choice food and sweet drinks" (v. 10).* What's more, the people were to "send some food and drinks to those who have nothing prepared." They were not to keep the joy to themselves; instead, they were to live out the command to love their neighbor by providing for those who did not have any with them.

What was the reason for all the rejoicing and feasting? *"They now understood the words that had been made known to them"* *(v.12)*. There is great joy in understanding Scripture! Just like the feasts after weddings, understanding Scripture is a cause to rejoice and share that joy with the people around us.

Does God's Word bring you joy? When we let His truth sink into our hearts, it can bring a deep sense of personal conviction and repentance. But it can also bring joy that goes beyond anything the world offers! I know I have that Joy, Joy, Joy, Joy... down in my heart.

DAY 34 ON THE PORCH

The night sky has always fascinated me. On a clear night, far from city lights, you see all the way to the Promised Land. I can remember as a kid standing in a field looking up and thinking, "My God, there must be a gazillion stars up there."

I sometimes forget how wonderful looking into the night sky is. It's magical. Constellations, galaxies, and Millennium Falcons. You should make it a point to see this. It's amazing! And just think... God put just as much thought into me and you as He did all that.

This is such a beautiful night. Some would say that the night sky never changes. Everything is where it has been since long before Samuel Leroy Jackson learned to cuss. These people would say that ancient Baptists used to tell time and dates by the stars... because they never changed... the stars, and ancient Baptists.

I suppose they'd be right... if you looked at it that way. But I see something different every time I look up. I see hopes and dreams. I see wishes, just waiting to fall upon unsuspecting wishers. I also see miracles. And that's why I keep looking up.

Some nights seem surreal. Almost like I'm not looking into the sky, but instead, I'm part of it. These nights are nothing at all like a normal night. This is the kind you can feel. Maybe it's just the quietness. Perhaps it's the Creator Himself making His presence known.

I feel sorry for folks who have never been outside the city to witness this show. They never get to see the night sky like it was meant to be seen. Sure, they have stars above big cities too, but they have to compete with streetlights, video billboards, and twenty-four-hour taco joints.

But on a rural road, in a field or gravel pit far from cappuccinos and hip-hop country music, it's different. The only competition out here is fireflies. And that's where the magic happens. That's where you learn to believe in miracles. Because surely, if a Fella could create all that, miracles are a drop in a bucket for Him.

When I was a kid, I would sit outside with my dad, and he would point to the Big Dipper. It was the only galactic reference he knew. Whenever he found it, he would show it to me. Each time was like the first. He would tell me how Indians believed in the healing powers of stars. And how they believed that for each person on earth, there was a star in heaven, and each shared souls.

He told so many stories about the night sky. Most of them were oiled with a six-pack of beer, so they sounded like nursery rhymes to an adolescent boy hanging out with his dad. And I never got enough of them.

Every now and again, we would see a shooting star. "Make a wish," he would insist. "Make it something good." And I would. I would close my eyes so tight, that my face would turn red. I would think really hard. And I would wish for things that made me smile.

"You know, it only comes true if you believe in it," my dad would say.

So, I would believe in it. I would believe in it with everything in me. In that very moment, I believed that anything was possible.

My dad would wish for overtime work. More money. A new transmission. More beer. I wished for all sorts of things back then. Big things. New bikes, cars I couldn't yet drive, enough money to buy the whole fourth-grade class an ice cream… and I even once wished to hold hands with Daisy Duke. I know it was farfetched. It would never happen. Three people in the fourth grade were lactose intolerant.

But still, I hung onto hope. I clung to the belief that maybe one day, my star would fall, bringing with it my very own wish. I never knew which one was mine, so I didn't take chances. I wished on them all. I didn't waste my wishes on unimportant stuff. All these things would change my world back then. I would close my eyes and think about these things. And there was always that question of "what if."

"What if" it happens? What if I get my wish? What if that star is mine? What if....

Deep down, I knew that boys like me didn't collect on wishes like that. We settled. My whole juvenile life was about settling. A hand-me-down bike and a Dukes of Hazzard poster were as close as I'd ever get to my wishes.

After my father died, I'd sit outside often and look for the Big Dipper. When I'd find it, I'd smile. I'd recall the times when wishes were top shelf. Back when I still believed in them with a youthful innocence.

Something happened over time. I grew older. Things get complicated with age. I had mortgages and kids of my own. Wishes seemed like something that I had to create on my own. And I tried. I could no longer put orders in. It was my job to fill them. Still to this day, I will do anything in my power to make my kids' dreams come true.

Occasionally, a shooting star will catch my eye... and I'll make a wish again. But cars and ice cream money never get brought up. My wishes have changed. I now wish for things I never thought of back then. Like my kids being healthy and happy. I wish for things that make my wife smile... like holding her hand and buying her tacos.

I wish for kindness. I wish for schools where bullies didn't get their way. I wish kids didn't grow up so fast. I wish that more parents didn't expect schools to raise their kids for them. And with that, I wish that teachers got paid more because until my wish comes true, a teacher is the best parent some kids will ever know.

I wish daddies took their kids fishing more often. I wish they took the time to look at the stars together. Not as a planned outing, but spontaneous and with no time limits set.

I wish we watched the world through the vastness it is, and not through a smartphone. I once saw a girl spend hundreds of dollars on a concert ticket to watch the concert on her phone as she recorded it. Don't get me wrong. If that lights your fire, I'm happy for you. But don't forget, there's a lot more life just beyond the edges of that device in your hand.

The sky is beautiful at night. I don't know why it stands out to me so much. Perhaps, God made all this just for me to see. I know that's selfish just to think that, but that's what makes it so special. Because seeing this the way I do, you start believing in things.

You believe that kindness isn't so far-fetched. You believe kids still have a chance. And you start believing in other things, too. You believe all those wishes you made long ago weren't wasted. You believe in things that were once just imaginary thoughts… but now… what if.

I believe there's a God up there just waiting on all of us to believe in big things. I may be totally off the tracks here, but I believe that things as simple as a wish are not much different than believing that God can make those imaginary things happen. We just don't call them wishes anymore. We call them prayers. And it's faith that makes them come true.

I believe that once we stop putting limitations on what God can do, He stops putting limitations on our wishes… and better yet, our prayers.

But I do. I do still believe in wishes. I also believe in prayer. I believe in the power of God. I believe the stars can be hypnotizing… especially on nights like this. I believe in happy marriages. Old cars and new boots. I believe in potluck dinners… visiting cousins and I believe we should always prioritize family reunions.

I believe that my dad was right: "It only comes true if you believe in it." So, I choose to believe. I believe in wishes, and more importantly, I believe in prayers.

I also believe in miracles. And when I look up, I believe that the whole sky is full of them.

This is the confidence we have in approaching God: that if we ask anything according to his will, he hears us. ~ 1 JOHN 5:14

John says that God hears us if we ask anything that agrees with His will. If God hears us, our request will be granted. This confidence motivates us to approach God boldly in prayer. Yet we know from experience that this cannot be a guarantee that we will always get what we want when we pray. Prayer is not a machine. It is not magic. It is not advice offered to God.

The key to whether or not God grants our requests does not lie in the form of words we use or even the degree of confidence we have that He can do what we ask. The determining factor has to do with God's own plan. The fundamental aim of prayer is not to get God to agree with us and follow our agenda. Instead, the goal of prayer is to subdue our hearts to the point where we agree with God. It is the spirit reflected in the words of Christ when He prayed, ***"Yet not my will, but yours be done" (Luke 22:42).***

These words are easier to pray than to mean them. We will only be able to pray them genuinely when we believe the promise of 1 John 5:14 that God truly hears us. He knows what we need. We can trust His answer.

DAY 35 ON THE PORCH

Prayer time every morning is important to me. It sets my mood for the day. I especially like getting up early to pray. I find it refreshing to sit outside, especially before the night sky gives way to the sun. Some mornings, you can still see the stars putting on a show. There are a million stars out some mornings. Maybe a gazillion. As much as I enjoy the sunrise, I almost want to delay it on mornings like those.

I remember as a kid, I would lay on my back and wish upon these same stars. If each star contains one wish, I thought I could make many wishes as long as I picked a different star each time. And just to make sure that these stars are doing their job, I also talk to their Boss.

I remember talking to Him in adolescent ways. I prayed for a new bike, or for my team to win. I would pray for an allowance from my old man, and sometimes I would even pray for better grades so that I would warrant that allowance. But over time, my prayers changed. They became more about health, and things that are important as you grow older. And as those things took the place of bikes and grades, the way I prayed changed a lot too. God became my friend. And if I could capture one of my recent prayers, it would probably sound much like this:

Hey God. It's me again. It is okay that I call you by your first name, isn't it?

I'm told I should talk to you like a friend. I call my friends by their first names, too. Somedays, I picture You right here by me. You're in overalls. You have on a cap proclaiming Your allegiance to the Crimson Tide. You are chewing tobacco and wearing Justin work boots.

I can picture you as someone I would call Bill, Harold, or Hank. Those names are easy to talk to. I think this morning I need a Hank. I hope that's okay.

Hank, I hope You never get tired of hearing from me. I like talking to You, especially in the early mornings, when I can sit on my patio and watch the sun rise. By the way, thank You for that. And for these stars. Man! I mean, Hank! This is simply amazing! And You did that!

I've had a lot on my mind lately, Hank. And when I first said I was going to talk to You, I was selfish. I wanted You to do something big for me. You see, I don't feel the best and I haven't slept well, but this isn't even about me anymore. I'm worried about a lot of other things. I'm thinking about people I care about. Some are dealing with things that make them feel so bad that they can't sleep either. But anyway... I know You're already working on it. I've asked You to get involved and I know You like that kind of stuff.

I'm reading your Word again this morning. I can't get enough of it. I want to know everything about You, yet the more I read, the more I find out how little I know. I want to know more about You than your cousins do. And even though I don't know a lot about You, I do know a little. I know that You're the sunrise like the one I wait on every morning. You're the trees that will keep it hidden until I wake up good. You're the sky over the property I pay taxes on... and over all the ones I don't. The smell of Sunday dinner that my mom used to cook... that had to be You, Hank.

You're a newborn's first cry and the look on a mother's face the first time she holds her child. You've done all sorts of things. And I'm not talking about big things—everybody knows You make mountains and oceans, entire universes and '69 Camaros. No. I'm talking about tiny things You've done.

The truth is, Hank, You do a lot of things that You'll never get credit for. Peach cobbler is only one example. I know that's your recipe. And still, I sometimes forget to sit down and simply say thank You. I'd like to say I'll be better at that. But we both know that I'm the world's most imperfect guy. So, I will simply say 'thank You' here. Thank You for understanding me, and for not beating me up for my shortcomings. Help me do the same toward others. Thanks for looking out for me when I don't deserve it. Thanks for today. And for tomorrow. And for all the other days You've seen fit to give me.

And one last thing, Hank, now that I have your attention. I've got a lot of friends that I care a whole lot about. It's Friday, God, and they're tired. If you see fit, please provide a good day for them. I love these people and they deserve a good day. They're my cousins.

I'm sorry for taking up so much of your time this morning, Hank. I know You've got bigger things to do. I'll talk to You again soon.

Can't wait until we hang out in person,

Your friend,

Russell

I have not stopped giving thanks for you, remembering you in my prayers. ~ EPHESIANS 1:16

In Ephesians 1:15–23 Paul provides us with a template we can use when praying for others. Paul begins by giving thanks to God for the Ephesians. When praying for others, we should not pray mechanically; we should give some thought to their life and circumstances beforehand.

Next, Paul asks God to increase their understanding. The Holy Spirit had already sealed the Ephesians *(v. 13).* But Paul prayed that the Holy Spirit would continue to give them wisdom and understanding so they would know Christ better. We can pray for the salvation of others. We can also pray that those who have already trusted in Christ would know Christ better. This involves more than knowing the truths of the Christian faith. The kind of understanding Paul prayed for affects the heart and produces hope. What is the nature of this hope? It is that those who belong to Christ are regarded as God's inheritance *(v. 18).*

The Christian's hope is the expectation that we will experience the power of God. This "incomparably great power for us who believe" is the same that ***"raised Christ from the dead and seated him at his***

right hand in the heavenly realm" (v. 19–20). We know Christ both by faith and by experience. Pray that they will experience Christ's resurrection power as they face today's challenges. Ask God to show how Jesus is ***"head over everything for the church"*** and we are ***"the fullness of him who fills everything in every way" (v. 22–23).***

DAY 36 ON THE PORCH

I love meeting and talking to people. It's a pastime that has been handed down through several generations that share my gene pool. I am not as bona fide as my old man, at least, not yet. He could talk for hours to someone he had never met and leave there being invited to a cookout.

But I am closing in on his records. I am getting better. Like a lady that I met in a Walmart not long ago. She recognized me from a past event. She attends a church where I spoke at a few weeks prior.

"I didn't get a chance to talk to you afterward," she said, "but I wanted to tell you how much your writings have helped me. And you do all this while fighting cancer, so I know I can push through my hard times."

She's divorced. Raising three kids. Their dad hasn't been in the picture since the last one, age two, came along. She tells me it's been rough. She works full-time. Cleans houses on the side. Her eyes show the tiredness of working a hundred hours a week.

"Have a good day," she says to me, as she walks away. "You're gonna beat this."

"Thank you," I say. "And I hope your day goes great as well."

"Me?" She laughs. "Every day is great. And one day, my circumstances will be, too."

I think about her words: "Every day is great." These are some of the best words ever. And then there's the ones that came before those... the ones that made me smile— "You're gonna beat this." Those are words I have hung on many times.

Did you know that using words like this is a commandment? It's right there in the Bible.

Hebrews 3:13 ~ "Encourage one another daily, as long as it is called 'Today,' so that none of you may be hardened by sin's deceitfulness."

God commanded that his people encourage each other because he knows we need it. In the Gospel of John, Jesus warned that ***"in this world you will have trouble,"*** which he then followed with a much-needed encouragement: ***"But take heart; I have overcome the world"***

When encouragement is absent, people will feel unloved, unimportant, useless, and forgotten. God knows his people need grace-filled reminders, so he calls us to encourage each other every day until his Son returns.

Recently at a job site—I'm going over something with my building contractor. A few old men had gathered on the porch of an apartment where we were doing upgrades.

One yells at us. "What all y'all doing to 'em?"

Curiosity is an old man trait that hit me around the age of twelve, so I know the importance of this question. I walk over to talk to them. There's an old man in overalls. The man wears a ball cap with a battleship on it.

"Veteran?" I ask.

"Yep. Navy," he proudly replies.

"Thank you for your service."

He shows me a tattoo on his forearm that reads: "Albert, Daniel, Sam."

"My three service brothers. Killed in action. I'll never forget them."

That's all he says about it. When he stands to leave, it's hard for him to move. He limps as he slowly gains momentum. One of the other men explains that this man is loved by many. He is always smiling. Always encouraging people.

Before the man gets too far away, he hollers back, "Y'all be good and behave yourselves. Love y'all."

Everyone waves goodbye.

"Love y'all." Those are good words. They contain the greatest word ever invented. Love. And the other word... "y'all". It's as southern as sweet tea.

You never need to remember names in the South. It's "cuz" for one. "Y'all" for two. If there's more than two, it's "all y'all." I once worked with a man for six months without knowing his name. To me, he was "cuz." A delivery driver brought his lunch one day and asked for Dave. I almost turned him away. "Ain't a Dave that works here," I said. Cuz came running for his lunch and set things straight.

Usually, I write for all y'all. But right now, I'm writing because a lot is on my mind. It's my escape. Even with everything going on in my life, words help me more than I can explain. And the words provided by all my cousins... all y'all, make me smile. I've heard words from you. Nice words. Kind words. And they help.

I believe in words, you see. I believe they do things. I don't know how they work, and I don't even care. I just believe they help and that's good enough. Saying simple words can make the sick feel a little better, make the overlooked walk a little taller, and make people smile when old men remember to say "love y'all". I believe in using words to glorify my Savior... and those who work hard, those who have lost friends, and those who feel invisible.

I'm a nobody from a small town that I thank God every day for. The people of that place are pretty awesome folks. I still can't believe they let me claim it as my hometown. But I believe it was in that small town that I first learned to use nice words. Because when I go back home, they always throw a lot of nice words at me. That's their main export.

I believe in feelings that come from words. Words that help. Words that may or may not mean a dang thing to you. But they do to me.

Words like: you're beautiful.

And: I believe in you.

And: Love y'all.

And: Have a great day.

And: you are more exceptional than you will ever know.

And: You're gonna beat this.

Words are amazing when we use them the way God intended.

"A gentle answer turns away wrath, but a harsh word stirs up anger." ~ Proverbs 15:1

Words. They can encourage or tear down. They can honor or humiliate. They can calm or stir up anger. James says this about the tongue: "Sometimes it praises our Lord and Father, and sometimes it curses those who have been made in the image of God. And so blessing and cursing come pouring out of the same mouth. Surely, my brothers and sisters, this is not right!" ***(James 3:9-10)***.

Learn to weigh your words. Guard your tongue and speech. The tongue can be a weapon of anger or an agent of blessing. Practice the art of listening.

"Understand this, my dear brothers and sisters: You must all be quick to listen, slow to speak, and slow to get angry" ~ James 1:19.

Listen to yourself talk. Are you negative and self-pitying? Are you critical of others and yourself? Do you speak before you think . . . and then wish you could take the words back? Do you speak harshly—and stir up anger?

Let God help you learn to control your tongue. Learn to use slow, kind, and soft speech, even silence, to calm you and others. To prevent anger from controlling you.

DAY 37 ON THE PORCH

"So how do you know, man?"

"I just know. I trust the peace that God has given me."

I was telling a buddy of mine why I was so sure I would waltz right through cancer and come out as good as thick-sliced bacon. It's not easy explaining these things. Truth be told, I don't really know. To know something you have to have some sort of educated proof. I haven't ever had an educated anything unless you quiz me on Alabama football, cars built before the eighties, or how gravity works when you're trying to hang Christmas lights from your gutters.

I guess this is not something you know, but something you feel. Knowing comes from the brain. But feeling... that stuff lives in your heart. So, I guess I just got a good feeling about whooping this cuss word.

"I need proof. I need to see something big happen," he tells me. "You write about miracles, folks overcoming bad things, and Mexican food that doesn't cause heartburn. But have you seen any of this stuff?"

Like I said, it's hard explaining this stuff. You really can't make others feel like you do... unless they've witnessed the things you have. Things like my senior year of high school. I had placed my deposit on my class ring. Big time stuff! Then, things went south in our little

153

apartment. The sewing plant where mom worked shut down. Dad volunteered for extra hours at his job. He picked up extra cash by riding the town garbage truck and emptying cans. Things were working out until he grabbed a can occupied by unsaved yellowjackets. They swarmed him. He fell off and broke his arm. Surgery. Pins and rods were used.

We went from a two-income household to nothing faster than a rabbit in a beagle pen. We lived on the income of aluminum can sales. And the day my class ring came in, I was embarrassed as I took my turn to go into the school library and tell them to send it back. I gave them my name. The lady handed me the ring.

"Try it on. Make sure it's a good fit," she tells me.

"Ma'am, I'm... I'm... well..."

"Is it not right? We can fix it."

"Oh no, ma'am. It's perfect. It's just... umm...I can't pay my balance.... and .... umm... well..."

"Balance? It says here it's paid in full."

To this day I still don't know who paid for it. A few teachers and coaches knew of our circumstances, but they all denied it. It was a couple of hundred bucks. That's big money. Huge money!

But that's a materialistic example. I don't expect you to change your mind over a class ring. I am not going to get anyone believing in big things over this stuff. So let me tell you about a buddy of mine who went through a living nightmare. His young son went through something so tough that God had to intervene several times. Two cancer battles. The family talked to Jesus daily. They became so acquainted that they would invite him over without cleaning the house first. One cancer battle is enough... but two? And on that last one, he met Jesus.

"My son's cancer changed me," my friend said. "And somehow, we have made something good out of this. Made me see how good people are."

And he's right. When Jesus called him home, there wasn't a cotton-picking thing he could do to stop it. But then, he went to work. He and his wife now raise money to help others going through this nightmare.

"When you drive through your hometown and see banners with

your son's name on them, it changes you. It makes you want to help others because you know what it feels like."

Something good from something bad. Something big is happening in that kid's name. If you need to see something for proof, I've got just the thing for you.

Big things are out there. Miracles are happening. Miracles don't always come in the form of Lazarus, or the blind being able to see, or gas under two dollars. Miracles and big things are out there every single day, happening right in front of us. We are just too busy to see them, or perhaps, new-age movies with special effects have geared us to the "prove it" movement.

And I can't believe folks are out there missing what I see every day. I almost feel sorry for the folks who can't see just how magnificent this short life is. When you finally open your eyes, it's a magnificent place.

And the people... people out there are responsible for all the great things that make this world move. I am talking about people who bust their gluteus-maximus every day so that their day is better. The recovering cashiers, the truck drivers, and the cooks at the Waffle House.

And it's not just people, but moments. Like first dates, and last goodbyes. And driving on dirt roads which lead as far away from asphalt as you can get. Most would say they don't take you anywhere. They'd be wrong. They do. They lead you to places that can cause clear minds and spontaneous smiling. And if you stay long enough, your whole day will explode with big things.

If you need proof that big things still happen, just spend a day outside, away from artificial air, microwaved meals, and CNN. God created a whole world full of big things. Mountains, rivers, trees, and kudzu. He worked hard inventing light and dark. He was putting things together so big that the universe took notice.

He was getting after it. He started gaining confidence. Things escalated on the sixth day of creation. God created birds, fish, and ten-point bucks. Possums, groundhogs, and labradors. Trophy bass just popped into existence. Hummingbirds were created. Then a few escaped too early and didn't fully develop. They became mosquitoes.

Then God said, "Let us make man in our image, after our likeness. And let them have dominion over the fish of the sea and over the birds of the heavens and the livestock and over all the earth and over every creeping thing that creeps on the earth."

Then the game warden drove into the Garden of Eden and told God that He would need licenses for all that, and there were limits and seasons... and messed everything up. It has even been said that it was the game warden who told Eve that it was okay to eat the apple.

The Bible tells me He made this whole world in six days. Then, mad at the game warden, he took a coffee break and looked over his artwork. Wide and deep oceans, dense forests, and mountains so tall they caused the pearly gates to lean. There were lakes, meadows, pizza joints, and Bryant-Denny Stadium.

"It is good," He said when he saw it all.

I didn't see any of those as it was being created. But I see a lot of it daily. And I know that somebody made all that. I believe it was God. And I feel like if He did all that in one week, He didn't just up and retire. I think he's still creating stuff, doing things, and making big things happen. And that's a great feeling. I hope one day you can experience what I feel.

I'm thinking about this world, and the fine people in it. And how God is using them to do His work. To make things happen. These people weren't around the first time God clocked in. But now, since He's the Boss, He gets to direct all these folks to do big things.

Nurses who work doubles. Teachers who attend the ball games of their students. Those who pay for a stranger's meal, just because. People who fly banners in support of childhood cancer. And I'll be dadgum if the Guy that created all this wasn't right when he said it.

"It is good."

It sure is. It's so very good.

And I've got a feeling that He's not done. We just need to step back and look at it all. Perhaps we need to just quit talking so much and listen. Maybe its time that we all just be still... and let God do the talking.

Today's Scripture

"Our God says, 'Calm down, and learn that I am God.'" ~ Psalm 46:10 CEV

These words apply to our quiet times with the Lord, but they aren't limited to that. No matter what your circumstances, you will face challenging, stressful times. Times when it's difficult to cope. That's just part of life.

If you have been spending quiet time before the Lord, being still and reflecting on his character and listening to him, then as difficult situations arise throughout the day, it's easier to take a moment, wherever you are, to be calm and remember that he is God. He is in control. Nothing takes him by surprise, and he will help you through this.

When anything or anyone other than God is at the center of your life, problems that arise can cause things to spin out of control. But when he is at the center, day in and day out, he will calm you even when chaos is swirling around you. You will sense his strength, his love, and his reassurance and that will make all the difference.

Is he at the center? Or just occupying a compartment of your life. Is he your first thought in every situation? Or just an afterthought when you are desperate?

Begin to give him first place in all things to make him the center of your life.

Does anyone enjoy going to funerals? These are never attended for good reasons, but out of respect, you go. But, for me at least, funerals jog memory cells that sometimes make me smile. Funerals remind you of several things. You recall the times you spent together. You think of how much you've changed. You wonder if you still have anything you may have borrowed back in '88. You think of all kinds of stuff.

And you also wonder if the person who has gone to see Jesus knew how you felt about them. When was the last time you had a meaningful conversation? Not just, "How are you doing?" Or "How's your garden?" But I'm talking about really investing in their interest. And better yet, did they know you loved them?

Not too long ago, a friend I rarely hear from called me. Usually, this call comes with a favor he's asking. I saw the name pop up on my phone and immediately went to the thought of "what does he need now?"

It was an unusual phone call. Nothing like the previous few.

"Hey, man. I just wanted to call and say 'hello.' I haven't talked to you in a while and wanted to see how you were doing."

"Hey bud," I replied. "How are you? How's the fam?

We volleyed questions and answers back and forth. It was a nice intro, and I kept waiting for the requests such as, "Can you get me some Bama tickets," or "Think you could let me use your welder." But those types of questions never came. He rapid-fired me with real questions:

"Man, for real... no bull crap... how are you doing?"

"What have you been up to lately?"

"How's the new book coming?"

After about fifteen minutes into our conversation, I reluctantly asked, "Is everything OK?"

"Yeah," he chuckled. "I just called to talk. Are you surprised?"

"Sort of," I sheepishly admitted. "But it is a wonderful surprise!"

A few minutes later we said our "goodbyes" and he stopped me before I hung up.

"Hey! Hey! Wait..."

Okay. Here it comes, I thought.

"I love you, man," he said. Which of course, I returned the sentiment. Then I sat there and savored the joy of knowing that my friend had called...not because he needed anything or had a problem to solve, but just because he loved me. I felt guilty for expecting anything else. Then I heard a message from God deep within my heart. Let me paraphrase it for you:

"I want you to remember how you feel at this moment. Your friend, whom you have known most of your life, has just called to talk to you... not because he wanted anything, not because he had a question about a decision or a detail of life, not because he had a problem to solve. He called just to talk, simply to see what was on your heart—because he loves you.

That, my child, is the same way I feel when you talk to Me—not because you want something, not because you have a question about a decision or a detail of life, not because you have a problem to solve. That is how I feel when you talk to Me simply because you love Me."

God says to us in ***Jeremiah 33:3, "Call to me and I will answer you and tell you great and unsearchable things you do not know".***

Another translation says it this way: ***"Call to Me and I will answer you, and tell you, and even show you, great and mighty*** *things, things which have been confined and hidden, which you do not know and understand and cannot distinguish".*

It is an amazing truth that the Creator of the entire universe wants to hear from you, talk to you, and have answers for you. He won't ghost you, put you on hold, or let your call go to voicemail. He will answer. He's been waiting for your call. In fact, He's been trying to call you.

He wants you to put Him first. Don't give Him what's left over from your time, but genuinely *want* to talk to Him. Putting God first can change everything about you.

"And whatever you do or say, do it as a representative of the Lord Jesus, giving thanks through him to God the Father." ~ Colossians 3:17

Consciously or subconsciously, we all tend to divide our lives into compartments and then prioritize them. God, spouse, children, ministry, job, recreation, rest, friends, hobby, school, Internet on and on. We try to be careful to keep God at the top.

But is that really what God wants? A top compartment? For us to decide how much time we allot to "God" things? Probably not. Yes, we certainly want to put God first in our lives. But not just in a slot at the top. We need to put him at the center, allowing him to be an integral part of every compartment in our lives.

When God is truly first, and at the center of our lives, he is in every relationship, in our business, in our job, in our family, in our ministry, in our recreation, in our hobby, in our rest— He is in everything that we do and say and are.

How about you? Have you given God a time slot? Or is He in every area of your life? Be willing to take Him out of the time slot and invite him to permeate every nook and cranny of your life. Make him the center.

DAY 39 ON THE PORCH

"Why God?"

How often do we ask that?

"Why can't I catch a break?"

"Why am I always struggling to get by?"

"Why do I have to go through so much, when I have been faithful?"

Why? Why? Why, God?

Perhaps we should have been asking "What?".

"What Lord, do you want me to do with this situation?"

Perhaps some mountains aren't made to move...

"But... but... the mustard seed? You know the story... Matthew 17:20-21 tells me that '*Faith as tiny as a mustard seed can move mountains*'. I have faith, but my mountain seems to be growing?"

Maybe... just maybe... your mountain is there for you to climb. Perhaps your faith is tested during the climb, but if you prevail, gosh, how wonderful it will be. Maybe instead of climbing, you dig? Maybe you dig deep inside yourself and soul-search the most intimate questions you have for God. And get this... He answers!

I think too often, we are not looking for answers as much as we cling to hope. If we have hope that something better is coming, it makes going through tough times easier. And if our hope lies within the foundation of Christ, our hope is strengthened by our faith. And during those times when we cling to hope, our faith grows, and we learn valuable lessons.

God could have "teleported the Israelites from Egypt to the promised land" but just think how much they learned on the journey.

God could have pulled down the walls of Jericho and could have rebuilt Jerusalem in an instant, but yet in rebuilding the walls and the temple with Nehemiah and Ezra, the nation was not only rebuilt but re-consecrated to the Lord.

God could have pulled Jesus off that cross, saving Him. But yet, would John 3:16 be a thing?

We as people often think about the destination we want to get to, and what we want to see happen, yet God not only knows and understands the destination but uses the journey to grow us closer to Him. We often find that through the journey we encounter more of God than if we got what we wanted immediately.

We live in a world of high-speed broadband and instant coffee; we expect results at the click of our fingers. We are losing more and more "work for what you want" mentality type folks with each new generation. Sadly, we don't really grasp the idea of 'partnership' with God, but instead, we expect Him to do it all. I wonder whether the popularity of 'revival' amongst complacent Christians is because they want to see God move... without them having to move themselves.

So, a challenge to us all, if God is giving you a spade to dig out of your situation, accept it gladly. God is giving good gifts to his children during these times. Those gifts involve the hope we seek. As we dig, think about what God is teaching us on this journey. What can I learn along the way? Maybe there is some element of apathy, or battle-flight as we find our way over, or through, the mountain.

If God is trusting you with a moment of growth, let's move that mountain a spade at a time faithfully, praising God for the joy and privilege of partnering with him. Will it be easy? These types of journeys are not made to be easy, just worth it. There will be hard days, but I refuse to let those hard days win because I know what awaits me. If you are asking God to move a mountain don't be surprised if he gives you a shovel.

And so, Lord, where do I put my hope? My only hope is in you." ~ Psalm 39:7

Is someone close to you struggling with a life-controlling issue? Perhaps an addiction, destructive behavior, or even an unhealthy relationship?

When a spouse, child, parent, or other loved one is living in the grasp of a life-controlling problem, the effects of that addiction or dependency will spill over into the lives that surround them. Most of us have known the frustration of loving a person we cannot control or fix.

Dealing with the consequences of a loved one's problem is doubly difficult. Not only is it painful, but added to the pain is the pressure created by our inability to take charge and make things right.

Are you a "fixer"? When you see a problem of any kind, your mind starts searching for answers. If I do this or that, I can make it better. Some kinds of problems can be fixed that way - but not your loved one's life-controlling issues. As much as you may want to, you can't fix them.

Have you tried to fix the problem? To fix your loved one? Fix yourself? Frustrating, isn't it? And that level of frustration can lead to overload . . . and all kinds of problems in your own life. And that is when our hope starts to fade.

There is hope. Are you ready to say with the psalmist, "Lord, my only hope is in you"?

DAY 40 ON THE PORCH

Following Jesus is not easy. It calls for us to become troublemakers, revolutionaries, seekers of change, and agents of transformation for justice and peace in the world. Sadly, some just choose to check the box of going to church and think that's enough. That's like buying a juiced-up race car and thinking you're automatically Ralph Dale Earnhardt. It just doesn't work like that. Following Jesus, the way we should require commitment, dedication, obedience, and four-barrel carburetors.

When Jesus called his first followers, he didn't choose strong warriors and wealthy rulers. He didn't hand-select them from the temples and mansions. He looked in the pool halls, the bass boats, and the Piggly Wigglys. He called them from among the peasants and fishermen of Galilee. He chose those that people could relate to more easily. He chose common people who wore hand-me-down flip-flops.

And what happened? Most were judged, condemned, and tortured. But Jesus commanded them to not return judgment, but instead to love everyone. Did He instruct them to believe that He would die for their sins so that they could gain eternal life in heaven, or did He call them to follow him into a more authentic and fulfilling life on earth? One that would eventually change the world by establishing love, compassion, peace, and justice in the unjust societies of the first century.

Was it about teaching his disciples an orthodox belief system, or instead leading them to a committed life of faith and servanthood? Instead of saying, "You knuckleheads will have it made," He told them up front that "this may get a little sideways before we are done."

Was it a promise of a glorious and placid future in heaven with all our loved ones, or was it about the in-breaking kingdom of God here on earth among the poor and outcasts of our society? His teachings not only taught them how to live for His Father, and be a servant to all, but to put one's self second to living a life that pleases God.

If we let the world conform us, we miss out on the blessings that come from living a fulfilling life of following Christ. Gosh, those blessings are never-ending. If we choose to look for the shortcomings in others, we will miss the blessings right in front of us.

Honestly, ever since I started to live more for pleasing God, instead of pleasing people, every aspect of my life has changed. And by making sure God stays first, oddly enough, He makes sure that all my friends, family, and even my insanely hyper dog are just as blessed. You see, I pray for all of them more than myself, and God hears and delivers. And I even pray for those who are different than me—those who are not of His Word, and those who could, and sometimes do, get on my last nerve. But I've found that you start to lose your own judgment towards people, you start to gain more patience, understanding, and love towards others because in doing that, it pleases God.

Matthew 22:36-40 says, "Teacher, which is the most important commandment in the law of Moses?" Jesus replied, "'You must love the Lord your God with all your heart, all your soul, and all your mind.' This is the first and greatest commandment. A second is equally important: 'Love your neighbor as yourself.' The entire law and all the demands of the prophets are based on these two commandments."

Since we were born, we've all been taught, and society has helped shape, how to get our own 'identity'. What's hard is that sometimes, this 'self-discovery' focuses on more of us, instead of God. I've been given a platform through writing, speaking engagements, and book sales that have let me shout about what Christ has done and is doing in my life. And I love it!

But it bothers me when I see people given similar platforms and never give thanks back to the One who can change it all. I've seen people more worried about how many social media "followers" they have than what they share on their pages. It's human nature that has to be changed through our hearts when our Savior lives in us. Without that, we become more 'selfish' in our thoughts, actions, and decisions.

We base and judge things on what appeals to us, and this essentially is what brings us to our own 'cliques' and friendship groups. We want to find other people who share the same judgment and thinking as us.

Now, once this newly formed group has established a strong sense of connection towards each other, negative relationships start to form within the group towards others who do not share the same beliefs and ideas as they do. When you run the race towards the cross, you will overcome your spiritual blindness and your heart will be flooded with light. The more you fix your eyes on the cross, the more you will begin to think of yourself less. And that is when you will see the true blessings in your life that God had for you all along.

"You may think you can condemn such people, but you are just as bad, and you have no excuse! When you say they are wicked and should be punished, you are condemning yourself, for you who judge others do these very same things. And we know that God, in his justice, will punish anyone who does such things. Since you judge others for doing these things, why do you think you can avoid God's judgment when you do the same things? Don't you see how wonderfully kind, tolerant, and patient God is with you? Does this mean nothing to you? Can't you see that his kindness is intended to turn you from your sin?" ~ Romans 2:1-4

Proud people are easy to spot. Something in the way they talk and carry themselves gives them away. How do you react to people who are arrogant and proud? What would you like to say to them?

It's easy to see pride in others and to condemn them. But maybe we need to look inward before we judge others. In fact, today's scripture makes that clear.

Although God hates the sin of pride, he loves us. ***"Don't you see how wonderfully kind, tolerant, and patient God is with you? Does this mean nothing to you? Can't you see that his kindness is intended to turn you from your sin?"***

When we condemn others for their arrogance, are we not being arrogant? Considering ourselves better than them? Instead of judging others, we need to let God's love flow from us to them. To be kind, tolerant, and patient with them. And we need to let their behavior motivate us to look at any smoldering arrogance and pride within us. To repent and humble ourselves before God.

DAY 41 ON THE PORCH

Not long ago, I met a guy through a mutual friend and heartburn. It was by accident. I thought I was meeting just my friend, Paul, but he brought a coworker that he wanted me to meet. It was Taco Tuesday. We met at a small joint for lunchtime shirt stains, and to catch up on jokes we cannot tell around our wives. I was ahead three to one... on jokes, not tacos, when Paul introduced us.

Let's call my new friend Joe. That's not his real name, but I promised him that if I wrote about him, I wouldn't use his real name, which is Chris. So, I'm sticking to my guns because I promised Chris I would. I never break promises, much like I never have grammatical errors.

"So, I hear you're an author?" Joe asked.

"Discount one," I replied. "Nothing like real authors with fancy words, designer dogs, and electric cars."

"Whatcha write about?"

"Little of everything— life, people I meet, the importance of proper fitting underbritches... you know... discount author stuff."

"Paul told me to follow ya— says your stuff gives broken people a little hope. Makes people think about life. And well, I'm more than a little broken."

"I didn't know Paul could read."

"I'd make you a good book. My whole life would be a bestseller," he tells me. "Just that there ain't no happy ending nowhere in sight for your book on me."

That's the brick wall most people run into. They're looking for a happy ending. They want the trophy before the race is over... the prize money before the game ends... the cake batter before it's mixed good. And instead, they end up with a beat-up tongue because the blender was still on.

Joe tells me he ain't never been nowhere. I find that hard to believe. But he insists it's true.

"Been out of state only twice in my thirty-six years. Once for a job and once running from the county peacekeepers. Neither turned out that good."

He goes on to tell me about failed relationships, dead-end jobs, and finances not fit for a stray. He says he has tried many times to turn things around. Even had a period in time where he had joined churches, hung out with positive folks, and even gave up the spirit water.

"Always slipped up," he told me. "Good Lord is probably tired of seeing me come back."

"Tell him 'bout your art," Paul interrupts. "Show him— Dude can paint sixteen chapels."

"You mean the Sistine Chapel?" I pondered.

"Yeah, That's what I said... sixteen chapels," says Paul.

"Ain't nothin' to brag about," Joe "*aw shucks*" it.

He pulls out his phone. He's thumbing through. He stops periodically, showing me beautiful oil paintings—sunsets, old farmhouses... dozens of pictures. Amazing work!

"You painted these?"

Joe nods.

"These are amazing!" I say, a little surprised.

"Just my way to pass time," he nonchalantly replies.

"Go back to that old gas station picture... with the old truck in it," I tell him.

He thumbs through again. "This one?"

"Yeah. May I?"

I took his phone. I zoom in and look around. It looks like a museum piece.

"You didn't sign this one."

"Ain't done. It's missing something and I haven't quite put my finger on it."

And... Boom! Got him! He stepped into his own trap. I had him in my sites. I explained that life works a lot like painting a picture. None of us are really complete. And like my new friend, many of us get caught up thinking about how many times we have failed, rather than the fact that we are still in the race, and what it takes to finish the job.

Sometimes we wonder if we have any chances left. We are as beat up as a run-over labrador and have no idea how we can go on. I'm here to say that as long as you're inhaling oxygen and can eat tacos, you still have a chance.

"Have you ever seen a half-finished work of art with a signature?" I asked my new buddy.

"Don't guess so. Ya don't do that 'till you's done."

"And you ain't done. You just spent a little time getting the base coat down. And when you let the real Artist finish ya, man, it's gonna be a work of art. You just gotta give Him the canvas and follow his lead."

Sometimes people feel that just because they slip up and commit a sin they can't be forgiven. We tend to find ways in our earthly walk to look back and say, "Man, I should have handled that differently". And it's a good thing we have an Artist who isn't ready to sign our little bare hindquarters yet. Imagine if the first slip of the brush, the artist threw away the canvas.

The mistakes? Yeah, they're there, too. You can't erase those. But He can paint over them. The prettiest paintings most often have a base coat that looks like a mess. But as it comes together... magic happens! Life with Christ is like that. It's about strengthening your testimony and faith, sometimes through trials, sometimes through blessings. Our paintings sometimes have stray marks, drips, and even spills. But if we focus on those, we will never see the finished product.

If we can put our trials and mistakes into our testimony and let others see our forgiveness, that's grace! The brush strokes of life cross each other often but blend together beautifully. Thank God that under all that mess, He is orchestrating something beautiful.

It's ok for others to see the incomplete you as long as they see the Christ in you. Once you stop "painting" and give up, there will never be a masterpiece. But little by little, you come together. And before you know it, you start to see it yourself. You're getting stronger as the painting becomes defined. God isn't finished with you yet.

Great artists sign their names *AFTER* completing their masterpieces.

If you feel incomplete, talk to the Artist. I'm pretty sure He has something in mind that, when finished, will be more than you ever imagined. And you'll feel more complete than ever. Even if you ain't never been nowhere.

"I don't mean to say that I have already achieved these things or that I have already reached perfection. But I press on to possess that perfection for which Christ Jesus first possessed me. No, dear brothers and sisters, I have not achieved it, but I focus on this one thing: Forgetting the past and looking forward to what lies ahead, I press on to reach the end of the race and receive the heavenly prize for which God, through Christ Jesus, is calling us." ~ Philippians 3:12-14

Many people begin the Christian life with excitement, expecting that everything will be different—immediately! They think that they will not have any desire to walk in the negative patterns they used to enjoy ... but that is just not the way it works.

Becoming a Christian means you are forgiven—not perfect. Receiving Jesus is not a "quick fix" for old habits and their consequences. Change takes time, and we can't rely on ourselves to make these changes. If we try to transform ourselves, we will always be disappointed. Transformation can only take place as we build our relationship with God by spending quality time with him praying and studying the Bible.

Are you a new Christian and still struggling with old habits and their consequences? Or maybe you have been a Christian a long time but things from your past seem to be pressing in on you. Perhaps you have tried and tried to overcome it, but nothing seems to work. You might feel like a failure. You've let yourself, others, and God down time and time again. Your past is dragging you down, and you can't see a happy ending.

This is not the time to give up and run from God, ashamed and embarrassed. Instead, run to him. Ask for his forgiveness and his help. Follow the apostle Paul's example. He knew he hadn't achieved perfection, but he put the past behind him and pressed on—focusing on becoming and doing all God had called him to. Learn from your past, leave it behind … and press on. Let the Painter work on you until He is ready to sign His masterpiece.

DAY 42 ON THE PORCH

W ouldn't it be nice if the adversity in your life could be evicted? What about those things that make your whole mood change when they pop up as you go about your day? Somebody cuts you off in traffic, or perhaps someone argues that Ralph Dale Earnhardt wasn't the best racecar driver ever invented. You get so worked up that words pop into your head that will cost you an extra twenty in the offering plate come Sunday. And those thoughts and words stay with you. You can't shake them. They become giants to you, that are hard to defeat.

The giants in our lives will take over and consume us. We all have them. Some are bigger than others, but everyone has something that just doesn't sit right with them. And it eats at you. It changes your entire day at times. A few giants will change your life. One of those giants is the sin of our past. We struggle to let it go. We question if we are equipped enough to do God's work because of what we did in the past.

And going a step further—what about forgiveness? We hold onto to hurt and anger that we say we have forgotten. Yet, we still get worked up over it when it comes up in our memory.

For example, someone wronged you long ago. You learned your lesson. You moved on. You distanced yourself from that person. You think you've let it go. Then one day, you see them at a store. You're angry all over again. You get so worked up that you drop your Little Debbie snack cakes. You relive what they said, or what they did, and what you wished you would have said. Your entire mood changes. You may have moved on, but you didn't forgive… and that giant in your life takes a swing at you every chance it can. You didn't move on… you ignored it. It's like a hole in your roof. When it doesn't rain, you hardly notice it. It's easy to ignore. "I'll fix it later." Then the rain comes and it's still there.

Did you know that you can lay that giant at the feet of Jesus, and it will never attack you again? The chains holding you to that giant will break. The battle is no longer yours, but the battle belongs to God.

In the story of David and Goliath, ***1 Samuel 17:47*** tells us that: ***All those gathered here will know that it is not by sword or spear that the Lord saves; for the battle is the Lord's, and he will give all of you into our hands.***

We can slay our giants when we admit to them and fully forgive… *AND* give it to God. Our giants will fall when we say, "Okay God, I've done all I can on my own. Now, the battle belongs to You!"

God commands that we forgive others and extend grace as we have been shown grace. It can be one of the hardest things we face in life! The pain and hurt others cause us is real and great. But the pain of living with bitterness and unforgiveness can poison your soul and destroy you. When we forgive others, we are not saying what they did was okay, but we are releasing them to God and letting go of its hold on us.

Forgiveness doesn't mean you have to be their best friend. It means that you have used the circumstance to learn, and sometimes, distance yourself and that you've forgiven them of the harm done. It's time to move on and leave it with God. It's time to face your giant.

"Get rid of all bitterness, rage, anger, harsh words, and slander, as well as all types of evil behavior. Instead, be kind to each other, tenderhearted, forgiving one another, just as God through Christ has forgiven you." ~ Ephesians 4:31-32

You may feel you can never forgive the person who has disappointed you and hurt you deeply. How can I forgive someone who has done that? The better question may be how can we not forgive him or her when Jesus has forgiven us for so much more? We certainly do not deserve Jesus' forgiveness. And yet he gave his life to pay the penalty for our sin. He gives us forgiveness as a gift.

Matthew expressed this well with the parable of the unforgiving debtor in chapter 18, verses 21-35. Our debt to God is great, and he has forgiven us. We are to forgive the person who wrongs us (a much smaller debt) just as God has forgiven us. All through the Scriptures, we find these two ideas connected: we need God's forgiveness, and we need to forgive. We are forgiven and need to be forgiving.

DAY 43 ON THE PORCH

One of the worst feelings in the world is feeling alone. When you feel like there is no one to call when you need a friend, or perhaps you feel alone when the world comes crashing down around you, and you have no idea where to turn. Being alone can lead to a road that is often paved with depression and anger.

It is easy to become complacent to the blessings around us. I've said more than a few times that every day is a good day. It's the circumstances within that day that make us think otherwise. While battling cancer I would sit outside and watch the sunrise almost daily. Some mornings I would be in so much pain, I could not focus on my Bible readings. But then, the sun would rise. Seeing that sunrise would change my mood.

But still, some mornings I would feel defeated, hopeless... alone even. Cancer will do that to you. I had a loving supportive family, more friends checking on me than I deserved, but still, in the quietness of the morning, I would find myself wondering "what if". What if the cancer gets worse? What if I can't work, and our finances are drained? What if... I die?

But God led me to a verse that reminded me that I was never alone.

It reminded me to fight harder and stand tall. It reminded me that no matter what I face, I am never doing this on my own.

"Be strong. Be brave. Be fearless. You are never alone." ~ Joshua 1:9

It changed everything. Still, I was having trouble finding something all the good in cancer, but believe it or not, it became easier. Knowing that there is a promise that I am never alone made me feel like I could actually beat this. I had many challenges. I've had more surgeries during that short time than I've had my entire life. But I still held on to hope.

And you! Let's not make this about me. I'm sure you are dealing with things, too. And you are way more important than me. People we meet every day are fighting giants. Some, we don't even know. They smile and say, "I'm fine", while inside they're as bent up as a sleeping deer in the middle of a country road.

Life can be full of challenges, sorrows, and tough decisions. But even amidst hardship, the Lord counsels us to be strong and courageous. Smile! Even when it hurts. And with whatever you're going through. Whether it's as simple as wanting a fried bologna sammich and being out of bread... or as complicated as depression, divorce, addiction — or even cancer... there's still hope.

I don't have it so bad when I think about it on the grand scale. I even think about you sometimes. It's not one of those "trying to solve your problems" kind of deep thought, mind you. After all, most of you, I've never met. But for all I know you are just like me. You're fighting a giant.

I even pray for the things you post about. I pray for your sicknesses, your worries, your families, and your cable TV when you post wordy-dirds about your internet provider. You tell the Book of Faces what you want us to know, but I'm sure you don't tell it all. I'm sure you're holding back so much it hurts. I wonder if you ever feel alone. I wonder if you hold back much more than you tell, and sometimes you just sit and cry when nobody is around. You're not alone. I know what this feeling is like. But not everyone does. People get self-centered. They forget what everyone else is going through. Some are quick to ask for prayer and short to give one.

Some people are obsessed with being in a good place. When it's not good, they lose their ever-loving mind. They want to feel so giddy that they become annoying. That's fine, I guess. We all want to be in a happy place. But happiness doesn't solve problems. It helps, but they're still there. I can smile and feel better instantly. I've even told you to try it. But happiness alone is asking for temporary relief. It's better than nothing, but folks, there's more to life than temporary anything.

Feeling like you have hope is where it's at. Being un-alone is something even better than happiness. I find all this in my family... my friends... I find it in you... but even more in my hope... my faith... my salvation... my God — the promise of Eternity.

I hope you feel that way today. With whatever you are fighting, I hope you figure out how important you are and realize that there's hope. More important, how un-alone you are.

But then, who am I to tell you anything about overcoming your giant? I'm just one little voice stuck in internet oblivion. I can't do anything. I tell stories. I make pathetic jokes. I write inexpensive words and put them together into horrible sentences. I'm nothing but a few insignificant letters on a screen. But I try with everything in me to put sentences together that make you feel something... anything. Anything at all... other than alone.

I use my cheap, one-syllable words to make you feel like you have hope. And some days, if I'm being honest here, they may be more for me than you. I'm sorry for being selfish, but at least I'm honest. But still, if it works for me, I know you can pull something out of it. Perhaps, something that helps you realize how important you are.

I don't know much about life—I know next to nothing. I've had way more failures than I have triumphs. But you'll never hear me utter the worst collection of words in history: "I give up." And I've got a feeling you won't either. I hope you find something that makes you smile. I hope your whole day gets better. I hope that while reading this, you feel warm, wanted, important, and brave — at least for a few minutes.

Maybe then, you'll know that somebody is thinking of you right now. And that means you're not alone.

"I know the Lord is always with me. I will not be shaken, for he is right beside me." ~ Psalm 16:8

Remember two things: First, you can't be brave by yourself. God can instill courage in you so strong that you will wonder how you ever made it without that feeling. Second, that's OK because you don't have to do it by yourself. God is standing by to help you. He is inviting you to turn your problem over to him. He wants you to know this is not a person-size problem--it is a God-size problem. He loves you and he wants to help you. And by understanding that, you will never again feel alone.

DAY 44 ON THE PORCH

"I can't go," he said as he stood and looked in the mirror.

His tie hung lopsided. It's not his fault. He's only worn a tie twice in his whole life. Once, when he got married. The second time, when he buried Mollie, his labrador.

"But Honey. It's your twenty-fifth-class reunion. You need to go see some old friends while you still can," his wife tried persuading him.

He has a past. He wasn't a good friend. He became a professional alcoholic and part-time cuss word inventor. He once pawned all the tools in his possession to pay his rent. That would have been okay... if the tools were his.

He spent most of his twenties living on the top bunk above a guy named Kevin. They shared a ten-by-ten room in a fenced facility owned by the county.

His thirties were better. He learned to weld. Someone gave him a chance. He got a job at a factory that made metal bunk beds. It reminded him too much of his friend, Kevin. He quit. He started his own business. He welded together fire pits and BBQ grills under an oak tree in his yard. One of his grill customers was a preacher. He paid him with twenties and Bible verses. They became friends.

One night, he wrestled with the Holy Ghost right there under his welding company's branches. The Holy Ghost won in round three. Later that week, he was baptized — twice! The second time, he meant it.

His business grew. He leased a building and hired employees. He makes utility trailers now. He still makes grills, too. He also makes trailers with grills on them. He makes a lot of stuff. Stuff that keeps him busy. Stuff that he takes pride in. Stuff that gives people a chance.

He has seven employees. Five have occupied bunk beds owned by the county. Two know Kevin. He gave them all a chance.

A chance—that's all anyone needs.

People change. People learn. They mess up. Sometimes they pawn tools that are not theirs. But that doesn't have to stay on their back forever. People judge others by what they know about their past. But what's worse is, people with a past don't let their own past go. They carry it with them like kitchen drawer clutter. They worry about what others will say. They set limitations based on their past mistakes.

He straightened his tie. He went to his reunion. He talked to many people he hadn't seen in over two decades. Small talk. Stuff about kids and work. It wasn't that bad.

Old friends showed them pictures of their kids. He showed them pictures of BBQ grills. What he didn't tell anyone was how he hired drug addicts and alcoholics. He's hired guys that live in pickup trucks in empty parking lots... and gave them a chance.

He didn't tell anyone at the reunion how some of his past employees had kicked their habits. He didn't tell anyone how he helped them when they needed it. He didn't tell them how he takes calls at 2:00 AM to talk to a guy who's bawling his eyes out. Then drives forty-five minutes to pick him up outside a bar and take him home. He didn't tell them about the night he found a man sitting in his car contemplating suicide. He hired the guy. He's now his best tig welder.

A chance. He gave him a chance. The guy took it. He had a second chance at life, and he wasn't going to mess it up.

He didn't tell everyone at the reunion how he starts each workday. He tells each employee, "I believe in you." He didn't tell them because it wasn't important. Their past is gone. Nobody needs to bring it up.

Now I want to talk to you. Yes, YOU... Anyone with a past.

Anything that makes you think you can't be anything you want to be, because at one time... you weren't. I want to tell you that your past is just that. It doesn't have to define your future.

Divorce, drugs, alcoholism, financial ruin, all the things that create a barrier for you... all those things can be the strongest testimony of your comeback!

If you are not given the chance, create one! Go for it! Be the best you that you've ever seen!

I believe in YOU!

As it is, it is no longer I myself who do it, but it is sin living in me. For I know that good itself does not dwell in me, that is, in my sinful nature. For I have the desire to do what is good, but I cannot carry it out. For I do not do the good I want to do, but the evil I do not want to do—this I keep on doing. Now if I do what I do not want to do, it is no longer I who do it, but it is sin living in me that does it. So I find this law at work: Although I want to do good, evil is right there with me. For in my inner being, I delight in God's law; but I see another law at work in me, waging war against the law of my mind and making me a prisoner of the law of sin at work within me. What a wretched man I am! Who will rescue me from this body that is subject to death? Thanks be to God, who delivers me through Jesus Christ our Lord! So then, I myself in my mind am a slave to God's law, but in my sinful nature[b] a slave to the law of sin. ~ Romans 7:17-25

Perhaps you have an attitude problem: pride, jealousy, impatience. Or maybe you are struggling with a behavior that you know is wrong: gossip, anger, broken promises. Or perhaps an addiction has taken control: drinking, drugs, pornography.

Habits like these have several things in common: They hurt you. They hurt others. And you cannot overcome them by yourself.

Perhaps you have determined to change. For a while, things were better and then you found yourself right back where you started. Today's scripture describes the struggle so well—even the apostle Paul fought the battle. But he also learned the answer: Jesus. Only through Jesus can we find complete freedom from life-destructive habits.

You might wonder why Jesus would be willing to help you after you've messed up again and again. The answer is that he loves you. Unconditionally. Recovery is a process. Developing the habit took time and overcoming it will too. But with Jesus' help, you can do it. And along the way, Jesus will send those that are willing to give you a chance.

DAY 45 ON THE PORCH

Things were going well. You had hardly any complaints. Your house was full of all the latest gadgets, electronics galore, and high-definition TVs. A nice collection of hunting rifles and enough fishing gear to supply the residents of Destin, Florida. Things have been so good, that you even have some emergency funds stashed away... everything that you've worked hard to get is all there.

Then, one day you get home and notice the door slightly ajar. You go in and it's all gone...all of it! Your electronics, your wife's jewelry, they found your cash stash... even your Dale Earnhardt die-cast collection is gone!

Someone slipped in while you were away and took it all! You're distraught! You're spitting fire mad! You're in disbelief that this could happen to you. Especially since you have that alarm system that you always turn on before leaving. Wait! You did turn it on, right? You go check the control pad. Ahhhhh! Dagnabbit! Forgot to set it. Someone caught you slipping and came in and got your stuff!

My friends, this is no different than letting the devil steal your happiness, your dreams, your desires... your Dale Earnhardt collection. He will come in and steal your employment, your way of life. He will come in and steal everything important to you, including your family!

He destroys relationships. He will cause addictions that drain your bank accounts. Lust, greed, and envy... he puts all that in your head. You stay angry. You lose friends.

But how does he do that? I go to church. I'm a good person. I'm a Christian and I have the shield of God to protect me. God protects us when we are a child of His... doesn't He?

Just like that alarm not being set, the devil will sneak in while you're slipping, and you won't even notice it until it's too late. You let your guard down. You don't pray as much. You don't spend time in the Word as much. You start filling your time with other stuff. You don't give Him as much, or maybe hardly any of your time anymore. The shield gets a crack and here comes that old devil.

He's waiting for the opportunity. He will come in when you're weak and take everything important. He knows that if it all is gone, you won't blame him. You cry out to God but in the wrong way... "God, why did *YOU* let this happen to me?" Well, friend, God didn't let it happen... you did!

Now what to do about it? You've got to take back what's yours! The devil is a thief and what he takes, you must claim it back. You first have to let God take back you! Obedience to God and giving Him your all is the starting point. Put Him back as your focal point and everything else comes back.

If he hasn't made it to your street, and that old devil hasn't slipped in, keep setting that alarm daily. Pray, devote time, study His word, proclaim Him as your Savior, and tell others about Him...... **LIVE YOUR LIFE FOR HIM!** We have a security system in place. Use it!!

The thief comes only to steal and kill and destroy; I have come that they may have life, and have it to the full. ~ John 10:10

We have false security when we lie to ourselves, thinking we are better than others or we are exempt from the same laws that apply to everyone else. There is no partiality with God. He will measure everyone by the same standard of His law. If we break His law, the same penalty will be applied no matter who we are.

People often depend on external religious behaviors for security:

- Being a church member

- Being baptized but having no personal faith in Christ
- Having Bible knowledge
- Being a church leader or worker
- Giving generously to the church
- Trusting in parent's faith

These actions lead to a sense of false security. We cannot earn our way to heaven. Jesus died to pay the penalty for our sins. We can only be made right with God by accepting Jesus as our Savior and making Him the Lord of our lives. We are made right with God by placing our faith in Jesus Christ. And this is true for everyone who believes, no matter who we are. For everyone has sinned; we all fall short of God's glorious standard.

Where are you looking for security? Your good deeds? Serving in your church? Your knowledge of the Bible? Although these are good things, they are not your answer. Jesus is the only way. Are you ready to commit yourself to Him? To receive forgiveness? To build a relationship with Him--trusting Him and following Him? Now, that is real security.

DAY 46 ON THE PORCH

I t stands out like overalls in Times Square. On all four sides, there are glass and concrete buildings so tall that on a clear day, you can see the Gulf of Mexico from the top floor. "It" is St. Paul's Chapel. The namesake for the church is the Apostle Paul of the New Testament, born Saul of Tarsus. You know the story of Paul to Saul... a story of transformation. A story of God's saving Grace.

Saving Grace... that is what St. Paul's is to even those that don't realize it. When the first worshippers at St. Paul's Chapel said their prayers in 1766, they might have given thanks to God for shortening their walk to church, though it was barely a few blocks to its parish partner, Trinity Church. But even a few feet shorter in a New York winter was worth it. George Washington attended here. He sang from hymnals, collected tithes, and parked horses. When the song leader picked a good one, he would holler so loud his wooden teeth would fall out.

Some say this is a protected piece of earth. Others would call it blessed. But one thing is for sure, they all call it breathtaking. When walking by, one can't help but just stop and stare. There's something that pulls you in... makes you forget your troubles... it's refreshing amongst all the craziness around you in the heart of a city that never sleeps. It's a breath of fresh air. Right in the middle of the concrete jungle, this place stands as a beacon of hope and love. It stands proud and strong. It stands willing and able. No matter what is thrown at it... it stands!

St. Paul's has a reputation for being stubborn. Incredibly on September 21, 1776, St Paul's survived the "Great Fire" which consumed Trinity Church only a few feet away. Hundreds of buildings burned. Every building within earshot was reduced to rubble.

When folks heard that the fire was getting close to the chapel, they came running like Aerosmith was putting on a free concert. People formed a human chain to pass buckets of water from the Hudson River to successfully douse the flames. They became known as the "Bucket Brigade". They saved it! While their own buildings burned, they found a way to protect the building that stands here today. That heroic achievement makes it the oldest public building in continuous use in New York City.

During the 9/11 attacks, it once again stood firm and was dubbed "The Little Chapel that Stood". It was in the shadows of the towers, and when they came tumbling down, everything within six blocks was severely damaged or destroyed. Not St. Paul's. It's believed that a sycamore tree in the churchyard took the brunt of the impact from the attack, but folks inside during the event say it was something else.

Outside this magnificent building is where I met David. He is a custodian here. I spoke to him only by chance. He was picking up litter outside the church when I noticed him. I interrupted his duties like a true Baptist. Ten minutes into a casual conversation about chapel tours and the high price of New York bottled water, I felt like I knew the old man.

"This place saved my life," he tells me. "In more than one way."

David was homeless on that day. He hadn't slept inside for two years. He forgot how to work a microwave, a television, and a toilet. His clothes looked more like tattered rags. On the day his world changed, nobody was being judged. He was standing and watching like almost everyone just moments before the first tower fell.

"I saw it crumbling and couldn't move. I was frozen," he says, recalling the day. "I finally got my legs to work and ran. That little church was the closest thing to me, so I hurried inside with about a dozen or so others."

The dust and suit covered them. By the time they got inside, everyone looked the same. They all had clothes on that matched David's.

"We were all just people. Just scared, crying people."

He said inside it grew dark. Ash and dust blocked the sunlight. It coated the windows. The whole building shook ferociously. Plaster from the ceiling gave way. He knew he was a goner... so did everyone else. Everybody inside was praying. He had never been the praying type, but he started repeating the words people around him were saying. Two of those words being shouted were "save me."

Over the next few weeks, the chapel became a haven for rescue and recovery workers at Ground Zero. More than five thousand volunteers worked long hours at the church, cleaning, serving hot meals, and providing comfort to all who came to the church for rest and refuge. David was one of the ones needing refuge, and also one of the ones volunteering. He realized that nobody knew he was homeless. Or maybe it just didn't matter. He figured he would stay here as long as he could make it work. After about a week, a parishioner noticed that he was there every day. He talked to him. They became friends.

"I felt like I was somebody again," he tells me. "When I said that prayer, and asked to be saved, I was being selfish. I was asking to be saved from that devastation, not from eternal damnation."

He points to the church. His eyes become glossy. "Man, He had bigger plans. He saved me... but in a way, I didn't know I needed. The church offered me a job. I lived in a little studio attached to the church and watched over it at night. I got a fresh start. A new start."

David is like many affected by the day. It changed him. It did something to him. He tells me that he would be dead if not for this little chapel stuck here between skyscrapers so tall that the Pearly Gates can use them as a doorstop.

Before leaving, David stopped me. "One more thing. When you ask God for something with all your heart, be ready. He's going to change your whole world."

"Yes sir," I reply.

I walk away thinking about that statement... He already has... I'm so thankful He already has.

"We can rejoice too, when we run into problems and trials, for we know that they help us develop endurance. And endurance develops strength of character, and character strengthens our confident hope of salvation. And this hope will not lead to disappointment. For we know how dearly God loves us because he has given us the Holy Spirit to fill our hearts with his love."
Romans 5:3-5

It is usually easy to rejoice when things are going well in our lives. But what about when we are having problems ... and suffering? The Bible says even then we are to rejoice!

None of us likes to suffer, but experiencing problems does not have to be destructive to our relationship with God. We need to trust God and see the good that can come through our experiences of suffering. Suffering teaches us to endure patiently. It also teaches us that our comfort is not the most important thing in life. Suffering builds character. It strengthens our hope because when we have to face another tribulation, we can look back on how God helped us in the past.

Although we would all prefer to be exempt from tribulations, God uses them to deepen our relationship with him. They are still painful, but we can be comforted with the knowledge that our sufferings do not mean God is displeased with us. And we can rejoice because God will bring good even from the most difficult times ... if we continue to trust in him and his great love.

DAY 47 ON THE PORCH

"What if?" Every single day she asks herself that question. She thinks of what could have been. She wonders how life would be now. I'll call her Annie, although that's not her real name. I met her at a recovery conference. She was your typical twenty-something-year-old with dreams and ambitions. But some of hers were forever changed.

She wasn't a bad kid. Not even close. She had just started college. She was living the all-American life. There was no shortage of friends. Life was grand. Then it happened. She was "with child." It was a shock. She was scared. She tried to hide it. Then she made the decision.

A few days later she sat in a clinic. They grouped her with a dozen other girls. She felt like she was in a holding cell. She wanted to change her mind. She tried backing out. She wanted to leave. The staff told her it was normal to feel like this.

"Everyone has these feelings right before they go through with it," they told her.

"It" was the abortion pill. Together with a group of girls, they felt pressured into taking the first of five pills before they left the office. It happened so fast that it confused her. She cried uncontrollably as she sat in the parking lot. At home, she followed the directions. She took the rest of the pills. She became ill. She was in pain. She was losing blood faster than she knew was possible.

She was rushed to the hospital. She couldn't call anyone. After all, she was hiding this whole ordeal. But now, she needed someone. She was fighting for her life... and one life had ended.

Her dreams changed in an instant. She had pictured a family. She envisioned a small house in a good neighborhood, where kids played outside. But to her... it was the end of those dreams.

"There's not a day that goes by..." she started to say. But that was all she could get out.

One more...

Let's call her Sally. Again, not her name, but not my story. When she's ready, she will tell it and it will be much better than mine. Everything was going her way. A student-athlete. Popular in school. She made friends easily but was as feisty as a ticked-off rooster. She would stand her ground against anything, and for anything, especially her friends. She was your typical teenage girl full of spunk and laughter.

Then... everything changed. She couldn't believe it. The test came back, and her heart sank. Pregnant. What would she do? She knew she wanted to keep the baby, but what would her parents say? What would her boyfriend say?

And what he said destroyed her. He convinced her that abortion would fix everything. She moved away to hide the pregnancy, only returning years later when any rumor may have vanished.

That was decades ago, but she still cries often. She wonders what the child would have grown up to be. She had picked names she would have given the child. She would sometimes sit up late and blame herself for a life that never happened. She reminds herself that she was forced into the decision. But still, did she fight hard enough? Did she do all she could to change their minds? Like Annie, she still thinks of "that day" as the end.

At that conference, I sat in a crowded room listening to stories like this. I saw hurt in the eyes of women who will never know the "what if" answers. All they know is that they wish that someone like who they have now had found them sooner.

"Sally" is now part of the organization that is helping "Annie". She speaks to young girls about choices. She isn't there to judge them. She knows what it's like to hide her choice. She listens. She smiles. She hugs. And she helps them forgive themselves.

The organization is Abortion Recovery Alabama, better known as A.R.A. Instead of picketing and shouting and hollering in front of clinics, they instead focus on recovery. They focus on those who feel embarrassed, invisible and shamed. The pain is real. The hurt is immeasurable. Some decisions weren't so easy. And some weren't even their choice. But these women live with something they wish they didn't have to.

The organization is made up of community leaders, churches, moms, and victims. They use biblical references to help these women heal. They remind them that total forgiveness starts with forgiving themselves. They love them. They show them how Jesus forgives everything laid at His feet.

I'll be honest. I didn't know exactly what I was walking into. But I'm glad I went. I heard stories of broken souls that are still wearing Band-Aids. But they are healing. I saw some that have gotten past their decisions... and now they are helping others cope with theirs.

They wish it were different. But it's not. They made a decision that they can't take back... no matter how many times they cried out to God to do so... some even offering their own life up for their decisions.

I don't know how I want to end this. I just know that as I write this, I'm thinking about my own kids. I can't even think what it would be like without them. A lump develops in my throat just thinking such. It's hard to breathe imagining life without them in it. My own eyes are blurry now.

And I realize that this is the feeling these women feel every day. And it never goes away. And if we are truly the hands of Jesus, we should love them, not judge them. We should teach them, not scold them. We should hug them so much that it becomes awkward.

I guess if I have to end this with some big shebang, I will fall short. If I need to make some statement that leads back to something inspiring, it's not going to happen. The only ending I can come up with is this...

It's not the end.

"But God showed his great love for us by sending Christ to

die for us while we were still sinners. And since we have been made right in God's sight by the blood of Christ, he will certainly save us from God's condemnation." Romans 5:8-9

Abortion has created strife that sometimes may spill over into the church. Those who are rightly outraged about the loss of life that happens with each abortion may not be sensitive to the pain experienced by those who learned the truth too late. Or the double pain known to millions of Christian women because we denied what we knew to be true when we chose abortion against our own beliefs.

Whether through perceived judgment or their own guilt, abortion made some of those avoid church. Many women feel like second-class citizens in church after abortion—caught in the crossfire of abortion politics and personal guilt and shame.

But God's ways are not our ways. No matter how others may see us . . . or how we see ourselves . . . Jesus looks at us through eyes of love. God doesn't hate us for our weaknesses and our needs. He knows we are frail and need his help.

Jesus can help you consider all the circumstances of your life and hold you in love as you think it through with him. Even if he doesn't love what you did, he never stopped loving you. As you mourned, he mourned too.

Jesus sees us through the eyes of love. He loves us so much he died for us while we were still sinners. And no matter what we have done, if we will leave it on the cross and trust Jesus, he will make us right in God's eyes. Jesus does not condemn. He forgives.

DAY 48 ON THE PORCH

I love mornings while sitting on a deck on my property. It's a good way from the house and overlooks a shallow valley. Surrounded by hardwood trees, as the sun rises, it turns this place into the perfect place to talk to God, read his Word, and soak in the beautiful start to the day.

Not long ago, I couldn't sit out here. The deck had become worn and unsafe. And for over a year and a half, fighting the "cuss word" had made it almost impossible to repair it. If I wasn't recovering from surgery, I was fatigued from cancer treatments. I tried several times to just do a little work at a time each time I felt like it, but it needed more than I could give. Removing a few of the old deck boards was about as much as I had accomplished over several days. It would take me forever to finish it at this pace.

I mentioned how much I miss sitting out there with a friend. That friend made calls. Before I knew it, a few friends showed up one morning unannounced and made my "God spot" new again.

That's the kind of friend I want to be.

Remember when you were a child and could easily identify your best friend—or perhaps even your "bestest best friend" or "second best friend." When one would get a new bike, and they let you ride it, you sometimes would promote them above another.

As we age and mature, we learn to accept and interact with a wide range of people. We have in-laws and colleagues and neighbors and acquaintances. But we still need friends. Proverbs 27:9 speaks of the "pleasantness of a friend." In fact, I often think the older we get, the more important friends become to us. It takes a long time to make an old friend. And while you can't usually pick your coworkers or neighbors, you can pick your friends.

It is no small thing to call someone your friend. Jesus, speaking to his disciples, said ***"I have called you friends" (John 15:15).*** He knew it was the ultimate compliment.

Exodus 33:11 tells us that, ***"The Lord would speak to Moses face to face, as one speaks to a friend."***

Friendship is a big deal. Friendship looks past things that we don't find as pleasing as others. Believe it or not, I've got friends that don't pull for the Crimson Tide. They holler for Auburn, Tennessee, Texas, and a whole host of others. Of course, I pray for their restoration, and hopefully, they will be forgiven for their shortcomings, but I would still fight a ticked-off grizzly bear for them. Because they're my friends and I love them.

One of the most famous friendships in the Bible is that between Jonathan and David. Even though Jonathan's father, King Saul, sought to kill David, Jonathan maintained his close friendship with David. 1 Samuel, chapter 20 tells the story of how Jonathan came to warn David that he must flee for his life—a fact that brought both of these strong men to tears.

Jonathan's parting words to David were, ***"Go in peace, for we have sworn friendship with each other in the name of the Lord".***

This God-based friendship would survive war and even death, with David showing kindness to Jonathan's crippled son after his father is killed in battle. ***"'Don't be afraid,' David said to him, 'for I will surely show you kindness for the sake of your father Jonathan. I will restore to you all the land that belonged to your grandfather Saul, and you will always eat at my table'" (2 Samuel 9:7).***

Friendship is a God-ordained and blessed relationship. ***Proverbs 12:26*** tells us that, ***"The righteous choose their friends carefully."*** God will use these carefully chosen friends to help you grow in your faith while at the same time providing you with opportunities to help them grow, too. You will be following the Apostle Paul's advice to "encourage one another and build each other up"

In *Isaiah 43:19*, God says, *"See, I am doing a new thing!"* God wants us to be open to new experiences, in our spiritual life and in our daily life, too. Friends can help you do that. So, take time to cultivate those friendships God has blessed you with. And pledge to make a few new friends! *"A man who has friends must himself be friendly"* *(Proverbs 18:24).*

"Become wise by walking with the wise; hang out with fools and watch your life fall to pieces." Proverbs 13:20

Today's scripture makes it clear that our choice of friends plays a vital role in our lives. Our true friends will not give up on us, and they will not leave us before the struggles have passed. They can't fix our problems, but they can hold us up. God can funnel his love and his comfort through them to respond to our needs. We can gather around the table with them with our chocolate chip cookies, our glasses of water, and the tools to build us back up.

Because when you've surrounded yourself with the right people, either nobody suffers... or everyone does. That's just how it is.

DAY 49 ON THE PORCH

Atlanta, Georgia— The Southeastern Conference Football Championship. The University of Alabama is here to toss footballs and swear words at the University of Georgia. Coming into the contest, Georgia is ranked as the top swear word tosser in all the land. Alabama claims they've done it longer, and better, and have the scars to prove it. It's sure to be a slobberknocker.

I'm here with three of my bestest buddies. We are already celebrating. There are going to be more people here than the entire population of Rhode Island plus three Walmart Supercenters. I can't help but smile at them all. I'm celebrating more than swear words and touchdowns. I'm celebrating life. I've gotten good news. Great news, actually. I'm about as close to beating this "cuss word" in me as I've ever thought I'd be.

At one time, I was close to being written off. I was told "This will be hard to beat", and "Sign here for your payment to be deducted from your life savings". But lately, I've never felt more alive. I no longer feel as if I'm living like I'm dying... and we needed to do something big to celebrate.

And these guys... gosh, they've been there for every step. They've held fundraisers, took me fishing, and told me jokes that our wives can't hear about. I wouldn't have one single doubt that these fellas would fight a grizzly bear and two Russian bartenders for me if needed... even if those bartenders were female lumberjacks.

And attending this game is like riding a barrel off Niagara Falls for us. We are nervous, but we know we may never get to do this again. And we are dressed in our best swear word attire. Hats, jackets, and shoes proclaim our allegiance to Saint Nicholas Lou Saban and his crimson army. One of my buddies even adorns a Grinch costume ready to steal a victory from our foe. But much like the Grinch, his heart has grown three sizes. He cares for others more than he does for Rice Krispy treats. The fella inside that suit checks on me more than the debt collections department at the cancer center.

I don't want to get all mushy here. I'm as tough as Red Man spit, but I couldn't be happier sharing this moment with anyone else if I had Dale Earnhardt, Willie Nelson, and Charlie Brown hanging out with me.

These are my friends. They are my cousins. They are who I chose, and they chose me. These guys are not like family. A family gets chosen for you. These guys are better. These are the people I have needed for the last twenty months. Because it's easy to find fake friends. They're everywhere. I have plenty of fake pals. I've figured out who they are, and they don't even realize it yet. Because I've gotten good at being nice to everyone... even fake friends.

And here's the kicker. I'd still drop everything to help the fake friends. I think I'd be no better than them if I didn't. Deep in my heart, I know they mean well, but they've just not had much practice proving it.

These people celebrate the big stuff with you. They'll even occasionally post lovey-dovey memes on your social media pages. But let the rain clouds show up and they steal the umbrella. These are your fair-weather friends. They're the ones that you haven't seen in months. They don't have time. They're always busy when you need a hand. They wouldn't go fishing with you if Bill Dance was chaperoning. But if they run into you at, let's say, the Walmart, they'll take a selfie with you and post about spending the entire day with their "bestie".

But not these fellas. These guys I'm with won't let me cut my own steak. I tried paying for gas on the way over to Atlanta and I haven't seen my wallet since we left Buc-ee's in Leeds, Alabama. It's being held hostage until we get home. Your fake friends would invite you for lunch and forget to bring their wallets. These guys I'm with would threaten you with a knee to your unmentionables if you tried paying for something.

True friends are God-given. They are the ones that you go to championship games with. They're like extra pepperoni on a pizza. Fake friends are pineapples. They're on the pizza, but you always wonder if they belong on *YOUR* pizza.

But I know these are my guys. We are having a wonderful time. We have met hundreds of people with a likewise affection for these events. We have been on television twice and it's not even lunchtime yet. My Grinch buddy is attracting kids as if he had ice cream dispensing from his ears. The other guys are laughing, taking pictures, and sending photos back to their wives. They are telling them how they'd rather be home with them, or shopping, or buying enough candles to cook a pot roast. That's what these guys will do. They will lie to be with you. That's true friendship.

I'm smiling. I'm having a grand time. And it's not even about me. It's about them. I'm enjoying watching them. They're like kids again. And we are all as pumped up as a bootlegger on payday. The game is still hours away. We haven't even eaten the first hotdog, spilled our Coke, or smelled sweat yet. And the most memorable part of the day has already happened.

Outside the stadium. A homeless man that smelled like Marlboro Reds and wet cardboard. He approached us. His story was one of like a hundred others I've heard before. Out of work. Hard times. It's not his fault—he's a victim of the system. He's living under a bridge. He's trying to scrape together enough to buy a bed for a night.

We listened. We are human, so we sin easily. Judging set in. Thoughts of "yeah right" filled out noggins. But whose job is it to judge others? Not ours. Grace found us. I gave him a few bucks. Nothing much, but it was something. The next thing I know, my buddies are digging in their pockets. They're handing him more bills.

He's smiling. I asked him his name. He seemed stunned.

"James," he told me. "The name's James."

I talked to James about getting help. We talked about possibilities. We talked for just a few minutes, but you could tell that he enjoyed any conversation... any at all. His eyes told a story of a hard life. Eyes can tell a lot about a man. He paused and looked me in my eyes. I was praying that mine told him something that didn't offend him.

"You... you guys... y'all are the first ones to show me any respect. Nobody cares about me... and definitely not my name."

"James, we do."

I asked James if I could pray for him. We all bowed our heads right there outside of the nation's biggest football game to be played that day. Football was an afterthought. And just like my situation, we were back to celebrating life. We were recognizing that football is irrelevant when you don't know if you'll eat today.

We prayed for James. What we said was between us, but we called his name out to the One that can change his entire life. With one hand, I held James's dry, dirty hand as I prayed. My other, I placed on his shoulder. An "amen" was said. I hugged him. He smelled even worse than I thought. His eyes were glossy. We bid farewells and from there, everything went back to normal. We were going to a football game. James was going back to begging.

And we all knew that his life didn't change at that moment. Neither did ours. But perhaps, a seed was planted. And perhaps... just perhaps... something else happened. Maybe in his... maybe in ours.

And what happened, then? Well, in Atlanta they say - that James's small heart grew three sizes that day. And maybe ours, too.

And then - the true meaning of life came through, and we all found the strength of *ten* Grinches, plus two!

"So Abraham called that place The Lord Will Provide. And to this day it is said, 'On the mountain of the Lord it will be provided.'" ~ Genesis 22:14

God cares and provides for his children. He is our heavenly Father and has promised to provide all our needs. In today's scripture, Abraham called God Jehovah-Jireh, which means "The Lord Will Provide."

We all have needs. Emotional needs. Relationship needs. Financial needs. Needs in every area of our life. God is our loving Father who will provide every need as we place our faith in him.

Some people have a distorted view of God because of an earthly father who did not provide for them. There can be any number of reasons an earthly father may not provide—illness, absence, abusive behaviors . . . and on and on. People may not view God as consistent because their earthly father was inconsistent. They may not grasp the constant presence of God because their earthly father was absent from home so much. People who live with an abusive or alcoholic father may not trust the constant love of their heavenly Father. Although an earthly father may fail as a provider, God our Father always provides for his children.

Many had a good father who did his best to provide his presence, love, consistency, and care . . . but no earthly father is perfect. And often circumstances prevent a father from doing all he wants to do for his son or daughter.

But our heavenly Father is perfect. Always available. Always loving. Always able. Always our Provider.

DAY 50 ON THE PORCH

I was in Hueytown, Alabama not long ago. This town is known for Kudzu art and NASCAR drivers. Red Farmer, Bobby, and Davey Allison, as well as a handful of other gearheads, called this place home. There are enough unauthorized emissions in this place to cause the whole state of California to sign up for therapy.

They live and breathe racing here. Folks have lawnmowers pushing three hundred horsepower and sixteen-year-olds stick numbers on the doors of their first cars.

But I was there for other reasons. My buddy was burying his father.

"He was a great fella." That's what people were saying. Those are the words that come easy when you don't know what else to say.

There are some who say things like, "He's in a better place," or, "He's at rest,". I heard a few say, "he's not hurtin' anymore." One older guy patted a fella on the back and told him, "Well, we know where he's at and it ain't nothing like the heat we have here today." Variations were all over the place. But what they really mean is: "We sure are gonna miss that fella."

Everyone found a seat as the lights dimmed. Tom T. Hall came over the speaker. He was singing one of the greats, *"Me and Jesus."* I like the words to this song. Tom T. has always been a favorite of mine. I'm jealous of his nickname, *"the Storyteller"*. He was an American country music singer-songwriter and short-story author. I will never be a songwriter, can't sing a lick, but if someone ever called me a storyteller, I'd smile so big an orthodontist would have to straighten my teeth back out.

"Me and Jesus, got our own thing goin'...
Me and Jesus, got it all worked out"

Those were the words Tom was hollering. I know it's not a Baptist thing to do, but I was tapping my feet right there sitting in the pew. And those words are all we need to worry about. That's all you need to tell anyone who doubts you, troubles you, or tries to make you do things you don't want to do. Unless it's the power company. They don't seem to be a Tom T. fan. But when you and Jesus get it all worked out, a restoration is taking place that will change everything.

Restoration. I like that word, too. I wonder if Tom T invented it?

In my book, "Southern Roots," I wrote a chapter titled "Restoration." It compares how God restores us, versus how people restore old cars. Old cars become dented. They have rust. Seats get torn. They smell like Marlboros and bad decisions. Then, someone looks at them and remembers what they used to look like. Then they start repairing it... making it shine again. Erasing all the years of wrong turns and spilled beer. Before you know it, it's new again. It's shiny. It smells like Alpine Snow. It's going to car shows. It's cruising the streets.

Our personal restoration through Christ is much like this. He takes us with all our flaws. He wipes away the dents. As we grow in Christ, we become less like the old body we had, and a new creation is made.

Look, I know I'm starting to ramble now. I've already lost the whole point of this debacle. And I'm sorry. I do that when I start thinking about things. Things like what I'm thinking right now. Things like when I buried my own dad. Truth is, it stings when those memories find their way into my eyes. Grief never leaves you. Some may even say it gets better. But those same people probably hadn't buried their daddy after he promised you he would live forever.

Grief is an odd thing. Nobody ever warns you about it. We sidestep the whole thought. We say things like, "he was a good fella". We should be more truthful to folks. Especially our friends. We should tell them that grieving feels like being afraid. Nobody ever tells you that grief doesn't always hurt, either. We just expect them to figure it out on their own.

I've made up my mind. I'm going to be a better friend. I'm going to tell folks the truth. I'm going to prepare them for the living hell that comes after burying a loved one. It seems as if my whole life has been filled with grief. As soon as I get past one, another reason piles on.

Grief and I are old friends. We have a love-hate relationship. To me, the weirdest part about grieving is that it comes in waves. Just when you think you're on your feet again, wham, another wave. Sometimes, I hurt so badly that I might as well just hammer my finger on purpose. Then, in a few moments, I'd be back to normal, hollering at the TV because my team was losing.

After the service is over, I want to tell my buddy the truth. I want to tell him that it won't be easy, but he will get through it. I want to tell him that if he needs me, I'll be there, but I want him to understand that it feels like total H-E- Double Hockey Sticks some days.

I want to tell him that he's about to have some rough days. Memories will attack him at work, in the middle of the night, at Walmart... in the self-checkout lane. I want him to be prepared because it's tough. He's going to miss his daddy so much he's going to bawl until he's dehydrated.

I walk up to him... and hug him. I look him in the eyes... and I tell him...

"He was a great fella. He's in a better place."

"Laughter can conceal a heavy heart, but when laughter ends, the grief remains." ~ Proverbs 14:13

Most of us have some degree of trouble admitting our true feelings and being able to express them, especially if we are struggling with life-controlling problems. But throughout the Bible, God encourages us to know our feelings and not keep them hidden inside. Jesus set an example for us: He had emotions and he expressed them. He cried. He got angry. He was sad.

We often hide the way we feel behind a defense to keep our real selves from showing through. Inside we may feel fearful, angry, or sad, but we hide those feelings by joking ... acting superior ... being silent ...

or employing some other defense. We may try to cover our sadness with laughter, but when the laughter ends, the grief remains.

Hiding our feelings can give them control over our lives. Unexpressed anger, fear, or guilt can have a destructive influence on everything we do. Hidden shame and sadness are roadblocks to hope and healing.

If you have been hiding your true feelings, has your "cover-up" helped? Or have you learned first-hand that when the laughter ends, the grief remains? Admitting your feelings can be a turning point. Be honest with yourself. And with God. And then with a friend. Being real will open the door for healing.

DAY 51 ON THE PORCH

In my pre-teen years, I loved puzzles. I can remember having several. I got a lot of enjoyment from those puzzles on rainy days, or when Mom contained me inside due to sickness. I think one of the reasons I enjoyed putting puzzles together is because my childhood was anything but easy, but these puzzles, they're predictable: No matter how long it takes, in the end, all the pieces fit. The final picture looks like the one on the box, the picture we were working towards all along.

Wouldn't it be amazing if life was just as easy? But when things don't go according to plan ... it feels like we're staring at a million-piece puzzle dumped out without a picture on the box. For me, this happened more times in my life than I would like. I found myself picking up the pieces of what I thought life would look like and questioning God. I just couldn't understand how a good God could allow things so good to suddenly fall apart.

When my mother passed, a day when I needed it most, I came across this verse, ***Isaiah 40:26: "Lift up your eyes and look to the heavens: Who created all these? He who brings out the starry host one by one and calls forth each of them by name. Because of his great power and mighty strength, not one of them is missing."***

Did you catch that? "Not one of them is missing."

While the ache in my heart still hasn't quite gone away, this verse brings me so much comfort. Here are two truths it helps me cling to:

1. When I look at my life and see only what I think is missing, I might need to remember my perspective is limited. Maybe my circumstances didn't turn out the way I thought they would, but I can only trust that one day the God who places every star "one by one" — and none are missing — will help me piece together the purpose of the hard things.

2. If I only trust what I can control, I'll never fully trust God. Remembering that He's the Creator (not me) and that He is in charge of the details, puts my heart in a natural place of surrendering rather than fighting to control something I was never meant to control.

For a guy who likes order and predictability, you would think these lessons would bring the opposite of comfort. But instead, I've learned to see letting go of control as carrying one less burden. Sometimes, I'll take it so far as to go outside and do what Isaiah 40:26 says—Look up.

When I do this, I'm reminded I'm not supposed to have all the answers. Maybe, instead, resting in Him and moving forward with what I know today is the answer.

I'm not sure what hardship you're facing right now. But I can imagine you are trying to figure out the "why." You're holding a million puzzle pieces of what you thought life would look like.

Can I whisper some hope to your hurting heart today? We were never meant to bear the weight of having it all figured out. But we are meant to trust the One who does.

"Never lag in zeal and in earnest endeavor; be aglow and burning with the Spirit, serving the Lord." ~ Romans 12:11

In the body of Christ, just like in a jigsaw puzzle, every piece counts. If you are not using your gifts and abilities to do what God has called you to do, you may be the missing piece!

There are many reasons we may fail to do our part. Sometimes we know God is calling us to do a particular task, but we are fearful. We don't feel qualified. Sometimes we get so caught up in busyness doing other things that our service in the body becomes a low priority. Other times we may be asked to do something that we don't want to do. Perhaps we feel we should be asked to serve in a higher position.

Sometimes we stop serving because someone has offended us. The reasons are many but the result is the same: We leave a hole in the puzzle.

If we don't do what God has prepared us for and is calling us to do because of fear, our focus is on ourselves instead of God. We can do all things through Christ! *(Philippians 4:13).* If we will step out in faith, doing what we know he wants us to do, he will make it possible.

If we don't do what God is calling us to do because we want to do something else, maybe something more "important," we have the same problem. Our eyes are on ourselves instead of Jesus.

If you know you are a missing piece in the puzzle, it may be time to have a look at the reasons. Ask God to help you get back on track.

DAY 52 ON THE PORCH

I had been invited to come to sign copies of my new book *When the Lights Go Out*. It was at a comic book store, *Izzy's Comics*, located in a strip mall in Northport, Alabama.

I was excited. It had been years since I had read a comic. As a young boy, I was given my brother's hand-me-down comics. *The Amazing Spider-Man, Kung-Fu Fighter, Swamp Thing, Ghost Rider,* and of course, my favorite, *Archie.*

When I arrived, I was taken back to the seventies— laying on my brother's bedroom floor, a box fan blowing on me, and a pile of his comics taking me on an imaginary highway. I instantly could recall how The Incredible Hulk battled Wolverine to save a whole city. I would read *Tales From The Crypt*... with the lights on of course. I would get so scared that my Superman underoos were in jeopardy, but I couldn't put it down.

But it wasn't just comics I found at Izzy's. Hundreds of vintage and remade toys got my attention. Action figures, posters, and even my holy grail of childhood... The Masters of The Universe Castle Grayskull! The whole castle! Still in a box! It was like seeing the G.I. Joe Aircraft Carrier in person! Getting this thing compared to getting a new bike... one that was almost new… with a headlight… and mag wheels with reflectors that weren't already broken.

I look around. My eyes are full of childhood memories. There's a life-size E.T.! I love E.T. There's a cardboard cutout that I thought was Brooke Shields. I put my glasses back on. Come to find out it was a scantily clad Princess Leia from *Star Wars*. I blushed. I knew I shouldn't look at it for more than a few seconds without getting a call from a church deacon. So, I didn't look… except a few times.

I could stay here all day and not see everything! There are football cards, baseball cards, Pokémon cards… Funko Pop… collectible movie pieces… tee-shirts! Even an original vintage 1965 pinball machine!

But as cool as the place is, the man himself, Izzy the Great is much cooler! And comics and collectibles are his passion… or let's say, *one* of his passions. Letting God control his steps is another passion. He has taken many leaps of faith in his life. Each time, he prayed over them and did not jump until he felt that it was God nudging him.

One of those jumps was from law enforcement, something he thought would be a lifelong career. Like the comics he now sells, he himself used to be a superhero. Working as a law enforcement officer for years, he routinely saved the planet from alien invasions and supervillains with mind-controlling powers. But more often, he would be writing speeding tickets and busting up crackhead parties. But still, he donned a shield that made him a superhero in the eyes of many. "To protect and serve" was his battle cry.

Tim, as mere mortals call him, started collecting comic books in 2014. Comics back then were more of a hobby for him. He would grab a few collectible pieces here and there at shows and shops, but busting the bad guys still paid the bills.

Before long his collection became impressive. He had many sought-after editions and limited prints that made people drool. He pondered the idea of making this a full-time business. But the risks of failure worried him.

His wife, Mellissa was proud of him. She encouraged him to follow his dreams. "If you love this, chase your dream! Do what you love! I believe in you, and I know you'll be successful," she told him. "I have dreams, too. One day I want to see Ireland. I want to go to some of the places my family is from. I'm not giving up on my dream. And I don't want you to either."

And he didn't. Well, he didn't give up on her dream, anyway. Another passion of his was, and still is, his wife. Their third anniversary was coming up and he wanted to surprise her in a big way. He thought about flowers, a nice dinner… maybe even a day trip to a nice resort-style hotel. But anybody could do that. Remember, Tim is a superhero. He's not just "anybody." So, he did what all superheroes do. He sold his entire collection to pay for a surprise trip to Ireland for their anniversary.

Mellissa was ecstatic! She hyperventilated, puked twice, and passed out. Then hugged him so tight he passed out. There they were, lying on the lawn, being called drunks by the neighbors… not knowing where this would lead.

Dreams are achievable when they start with "once upon a time," as theirs did. And when the lovebirds got home from Ireland, Tim started his collection again. He started small. He picked up a few comics here and there. He found out he was pretty good at trading. He could take a common comic and trade up until he had something that required hard plastic protection. For instance, he could turn a one-dollar comic into something he had to insure within a few trades.

Before long, his collection was bigger than before. In 2019, Melissa convinced him to take the leap and leave law enforcement to sell comics full-time. Stability was something that was hard to leave… but he did it. He turned his garage into his office and warehouse. He started working with artists and having exclusives done, with covers made just for Izzy's. His first big-time exclusive was *Marvel's Star Wars: War of the Bounty Hunters*. Tim smiled so big he strained both jaw muscles and still has an eye twitch to this day.

He began selling, buying, and trading so much that UPS had a dedicated truck just for his garage. Neighbors thought they were smuggling guns, drugs… or even worse…. bootlegged pop-country CDs. After running Izzy's out of his garage for a couple of years, the H.O.A. had seen enough. That and with a little convincing from the wife, Tim packed up and moved to town.

Brick and mortar. Something just a couple of years ago seemed farfetched. But they were here… but the growth didn't stop. Just two months in, the walls were stretched. There wasn't enough room for the talking Yoda that was just received. Again, they moved. Larger place… better displays and more toys. Tim's dream had become a reality, even reaching beyond his vision.

Since then, there have been more collectibles, more cards, and of course, many more comics. Like one of the most notable comics in the store, the one which held the first appearance of the bat mobile from the 1940s. People come in all giddy… asking if they can get photos of them holding it.

Izzy's has grown from a single filing cabinet hobby to a major player in the comic world. All because of one superhero's dream, an encouraging wife, their passion, and a few mean letters from the H.O.A.

It's a story that should inspire other dreamers… dreamers that know that there's success waiting for them if they chase after it. When you have a passion for something, it can lead to amazing things. You just have to trust the One that you have asked to guide your steps. It's like standing on the edge of a tall building and hoping you don't fall. But then again… what if you fly?

After all… superheroes fly all the time. Just ask Izzy… if you can catch him. He's pretty busy these days. What's he doing?

Flying!

"And now, dear brothers and sisters, one final thing. Fix your thoughts on what is true, and honorable, and right, and pure, and lovely, and admirable. Think about things that are excellent and worthy of praise. Keep putting into practice all you learned and received from me—everything you heard from me and saw me doing. Then the God of peace will be with you." ~ Philippians 4:8–9

Many of us have passion—the object of strong desire. Passion can be either a positive or negative influence in our lives. Hopeless passion may say this: "I allow my emotions to rule my actions and perspectives of my relationships and circumstances." This person is controlled by a roller coaster of emotions.

Hopeful passion may say this: "I love the beauty in the world and appreciate the richness of the relationships and blessings I have." This perspective can be more difficult to maintain but results in a better life.

Passion can be full of hope and joyful expectancy . . . or result in a sense of hopelessness. Passion can either propel us into healthy relationships . . . or push us into isolation. Hopeful passion helps us set goals and believe that with God's help, we can reach them. Hopeless passion makes it difficult for us to believe we can ever reach our goals.

When things are going well, hopeful passion makes us rejoice and focus on our blessings. Hopeless passion says, "This is too good to be true" or "This won't last."

Hopeful passion may reflect on the past or be hopeful about the future but is content in the now. Hopeless passion believes more in the past than in the present or future and so conjures up hopelessness in the now. This mindset is based primarily on feelings, not necessarily on truth.

Some passionate people live out joyful expressions of life while others live in a melancholy world full of disappointments and disillusions. What makes the difference? Part of the answer lies in today's scripture... with the peace of God with you.

DAY 53 ON THE PORCH

Don't take this the wrong way, but I don't want to be like you. It's not that I don't like the way you are. In fact, I love you just the way God made you. Sure, you may have a few flaws, like overspending, using unapproved Baptist words or even yelling War Eagle, but I can look past those. I still care a good bit for you. I just don't want to be like you.

You see, I have my own flaws. A bunch of 'em. But, I also have my own talents. You should see me get after a bowl of nanner puddin'. If I get caught up wanting to be like you, the gifts God gave me may go to waste.

Everyone has certain talents or God-given gifts that they are skilled in. For example, some people are very hospitable and relatable and know how to make people feel comfortable. Some individuals are talented businesspeople, teachers, musicians, or parents. These talents can be more than hobbies or even careers. These gifts can be used for the glory of God. Using your talents for God can allow you to be a part of advancing the kingdom of God, helping others, and improving the world around you.

James 1:17 tells us that every gift is from God. We all have different talents and God-given gifts, but they are all important and can be used for God's kingdom. God gives each person gifts, strengths, and opportunities. When we envy others, we doubt God's wisdom, minimize our own gifts, and long to be someone we aren't meant to be.

Look for opportunities to serve God and use your gifts in your daily life. Using your talents for God might not look the same every day. Some days you may notice exactly how God is working through your talents; other days it may be more behind closed doors, and you may not see how your gift is affecting others.

Even if you do not see how your talent is making an impact, it is important to let yourself be used by God because you may never know how you affected someone's life. And it's just as important to not try to be like someone else. Be you! God made you unique for a reason.

Today, let's concentrate on our own gifts and ask God to use them fully for His purposes. And while you're at it, throw in an act of random kindness for someone. Trust me on this one... it will make you smile as much as them.

"In his grace, God has given us different gifts for doing certain things well. So if God has given you the ability to prophesy, speak out with as much faith as God has given you. If your gift is serving others, serve them well. If you are a teacher, teach well. If your gift is to encourage others, be encouraging. If it is giving, give generously. If God has given you leadership ability, take the responsibility seriously. And if you have a gift for showing kindness to others, do it gladly." ~ Romans 12:6-8

God has equipped us to accomplish his unique plan and purpose for us. Today's scripture passage indicates how he wires each of us uniquely to have passion for various ways to serve.

When you are serving God using the gifts he has given you, your passion will grow. You will be excited about what he is doing through you. If you prophesy, speak out with faith. If one of your gifts is serving, serve well. Be enthusiastic! If you are a teacher, teach well. Be diligent and caring. If your gift is giving, give generously and cheerfully. Remember, God loves a cheerful giver. Has God given you leadership ability? Don't run from it. Assume that responsibility seriously, trusting God to help you. If your gift is for showing kindness, do it gladly. You may be surprised how many people God will place in your path who need that special touch of kindness.

Jesus had a holy passion for the cross to free us from the power of sin. What motivated that passion? Love. Don't just pretend to love others. Really love them. Hate what is wrong. Hold tightly to what is good. Love each other with genuine affection and take delight in honoring each other.

DAY 54 ON THE PORCH

Things haven't been all cake and banana pudding over the last few years for me. It's been downright hard some days. Like the days when my body aches like a sixty-five-year-old logger with a bad back. It's not always like this. Some days I only hurt like a sixty-year-old logger with a headache. But I've learned not to let those days hold me back. I've been through these times before and I know that it's only a season.

When my mom was still with us, I would do my best to make her bad days better. Dementia ate at her until almost every day was bad. But we would talk. We would recall memories. I would bring her some of her favorite things: pear salad, cornbread and buttermilk, and her Bible.

No matter how bad a day she was having, she would still find a way to smile. And that's what I try to do. Her bravery was far exceeding anything I could ever muster, but every day, I remember to smile because of her.

I remember her last days. She slept constantly. She became nonverbal. For days she hadn't said anything. Then, one day I walked in and her eyes were open and she had the biggest smile on her face.

"I love you," she whispered.

I lost it. I was crying like an onion cutter in a Mexican joint. I said those words back to her while trying to control my sobbing.

"Everything is going to be alright," she said. "The man told me I was going to be fine."

"What man, Mom?"

"I asked him his name. It was Jesus."

Mom held on for a few more days. Then one Saturday morning in October, the Man came and took her home. And she was fine again. Everything was okay, just like He had promised. And I will be, too. I'll be better than that. One day, I won't hurt. I'll have energy again. Who knows, maybe I'll even be a better writer. In all honesty, I still can't believe people even call me that.

And if you are torturing yourself by reading this horrible collection of bad grammar, I want to remind you that one day, things will be better for you, too. You're going to be okay. You're going to smile. Maybe even laugh because what you went through was worth it. That's not just my opinion. It's my belief. It's not a little quote that you read on a T-shirt or meme. It's my honest-to-goodness belief that you'll be okay.

You really are going to make it through this mess you're going through. Just try to forget what others tell you and believe in better days yourself. You don't have to say some magical words, speak to the Boss in Latin, Hebrew, or Hillbilly. You just have to believe that He is already working on the hellish situation that keeps you up at night.

I know it's hard to believe it right now. But this writer—still can't believe you call me that—is telling you straight up, that things will get better. Things are bad. You haven't felt like this since they canceled Happy Days. But even you know that there's something inside of you that is telling you I'm right. It may be a gut feeling. It may be a dream. It could be a small, very faint voice. Almost a whisper. But it's there. That voice may be saying, "Ya know, this writer has a point." Even the voice is calling me that now. Never in a million years would I have thought that.

But here's the thing. It doesn't matter what I think. I have been insignificant my whole life. I guess that's why I became a writer. Being a writer is what's left over after the important things are given away to people with meaningful credentials. But what I say doesn't matter. But that voice... listen to the voice.

It will tell you things that will put you back on track. It will say things like, "You're smart. You're pretty. You're better than you think. Don't give up. Don't worry, you won't ever have to be a writer."

If you listen to the voice that's trying to call out to you, you'll start believing that things will be better. "You're important," the voice will say. "Your miracle is on the way." And if you keep listening, the voice will tell you that everything will be okay, even on the days when you ache like a logger.

At this point, you probably think I've lost it. You're thinking, "Man, this idiot doesn't even know me. How's he gonna tell me it will be alright?" And that's okay. I've been called worse than an idiot. Even the voice is calling me a writer, so you can't hurt my feelings.

I know it's hard to believe. You've been praying for months. Nothing has happened. You're wondering if anyone is listening. Things haven't gotten any better. In fact, some days feel even worse. But you just have to trust me. These things don't happen overnight. Sometimes, they don't happen at all—it's even better.

Every now and again, your prayer doesn't get answered because you didn't pray for big enough things. You just want the pain to go away, so that's what you pray for. But the Creator of the universe has bigger plans. He wants to heal you altogether.

One day you'll wake up and you won't hurt. You'll smile. And you'll whisper words like, "I love you." And you'll hear them back. One day, the sky will seem bluer. The air will smell like gardenias. Hot wings won't cause heartburn. Nobody will rap a country song again. Your transmission isn't busted anymore.

And you'll start believing in that little voice inside you. You'll even believe that the writer was right. And that is big. Very few times in this writer's life has he been right about anything. But the voice is always right. And the voice loves you so much that it would never lie to you.

And if you find it hard to believe me... some dime store writer with nickel books, that's okay. I'm not the one you should believe in anyway. But just do this for me... ask the voice who He is.

"Rejoice in our confident hope. Be patient in trouble, and keep on praying." Romans 12:12

Passion to serve God is an amazing thing. Passion to accomplish what He has called us to do is an amazing thing. Our passionate service must be motivated by love. Love for God. Love for others. The kind of love that motivated Jesus to suffer and die on the cross to pay the price for our sins. And to achieve that, we must talk to God daily. We must pray, trust, and grow.

Sadly, we are sometimes motivated by other things. A desire for attention or wanting people to show their gratitude. The feeling of power. Trying to "earn points" with God. Or a multitude of other selfish motives. We forget to talk to Him unless we need something.

People of great passion can fall prey to stress, anger, depression, and despair. They may develop an "I don't care" attitude—especially when they are focused on what is wrong in life rather than on what is right and what God is doing to make things right. Passionate people can find themselves in dark places at times.

We can get off track when things do not go the way we expect them to or when people fail us in ways that are hurtful or upsetting. It's especially easy for that to happen when we are motivated by anything other than love. And without that prayer life, we spiral into depression, anger, and turmoil.

When this happens, we need to take a step back and ask God to get us back on track and reveal if we have any wrong motives. To help us have the right attitude. As today's scripture says, we need to be comforted by God's ultimate plan for our life, to be patient and always prayerful. Sometimes, we just need to pray… and listen to the Voice.

DAY 55 ON THE PORCH

Being on social media means that all my readers have access to message me. I actually enjoy the messages I get from people I have never met. I have become long-distance cousins with many of them. Like the one I received not long ago.

"You don't know me, but I've been following you for a while. Your writings have made me think a lot. I hardly ever read the Bible, but you write stuff that has made me want to. I've started reading some. Not every day, but I'm trying. Anyway, just wanted to say thanks. I'm working on myself. I need to clean up my act so maybe Jesus will take me back. Take care."

Second message: "Forgot to tell you but even though I ain't where I need to be, and don't know if God hears me, but I pray for you and your healing. I haven't always done that."

We carried on a conversation through messenger after he reached out to me. His name and the rest of our talk aren't important to anyone but us. But it got me thinking. How many other people believe that you have to get dressed up to go see Jesus? He loves us coming by, even if it's in our old work clothes. In fact, He even wants us to come as we are. Because He loves us.

Everything that Jesus did for us, he did out of love. The Bible says that God made you to love you. The only reason you're alive is because you were made to be loved by God. If God didn't want you alive, your heart would stop instantly; you wouldn't even be breathing right now. You wouldn't have to endure this grammatical mess you're reading. But you are. So that must mean something.

What it means is God made you and wants you alive so he can love you and so you can love him back. That's a fact! That's not my opinion. That's not a guess. That's the honest truth. God didn't just say he loved you; he showed it. The Bible says, ***"God showed his great love for us by sending Christ to die for us while we were still sinners" (Romans 5:8)***. It says while we were still sinners. Before I even knew God or knew I needed God in my life, Jesus died for me.

There's a myth that says we have to clean up our act before we can come to God: "I've got to get it all together. There are a few things I've got to get right in my life first, and then I'll come to God." No! You come to God with your problems — the good, the bad, the ugly... all of it. Don't wash your car. Don't get dressed up. Don't practice what you'll say when you're ready... just come. He's already making you a bologna sammich and waiting on you.

It's like when we brush our teeth before we go to the dentist to have our teeth cleaned or when we wash the dishes before we put them in the dishwasher. Why do we do this? God says, "No, no! You don't have to clean up your act. Just bring it all to me. Bring me all your problems. I have all the answers. Come as you are."

The Bible says, ***"He will send down help from heaven to save me because of his love" (Psalm 57:3)***. He sent himself from Heaven to save us because of his love. So, you can bring your problems to God because he has the answer. If you don't act on this news, then the death of Jesus Christ and his Resurrection are wasted for you personally. It makes no difference in your life. You may recognize the gift, but you still have to receive it.

"You will be saved, if you honestly say, 'Jesus is Lord,' and if you believe with all your heart that God raised him from death. God will accept you and save you, if you truly believe this and tell it to others" ~ Romans 10:9-10

God is not asking you to make a promise you cannot keep. God is asking you to believe a promise that only he can keep. If you feel like something is missing in your life, I promise you, it's not my awful writing that will fill that need. It's the Word of God and a relationship with Jesus Christ that will get you as pumped up as a Powerball winner.

Getting your act together before you invite Him over... hogwash! If we were already squeaky clean, we would put the Dude out of business. He's waiting... get out of the shower and go see Him.

"But God showed his great love for us by sending Christ to die for us while we were still sinners." Romans 5:8

Have you ever felt as though you could earn God's love? Today's scripture points out that God loves us so much he sent Christ to die for us while we were still sinners. Jesus suffered and died on the cross to pay the price for our sins. Because we deserved it? Absolutely not. He did it because of his great love for us.

God saved you by his grace when you believed. And you can't take credit for this; it is a gift from God. ~ Ephesians 2:8

We can never do enough to earn his forgiveness and love. He already loves us more than we can begin to comprehend. We just need to believe. To accept his gift of love.

After we become Christians, we may still do things for God so he will continue loving us. Or so he will love us more. But the Bible teaches us he will always love us.

Can anything ever separate us from Christ's love? Does it mean he no longer loves us if we have trouble or calamity, or are persecuted, or hungry, or destitute, or in danger, or threatened with death? (As the Scriptures say, "For your sake we are killed every day; we are being slaughtered like sheep.") No, despite all these things, overwhelming victory is ours through Christ, who loved us.

And I am convinced that nothing can ever separate us from God's love. Neither death nor life, neither angels nor demons, neither our fears for today nor our worries about tomorrow— not even the powers of hell can separate us from God's love. No power in the sky above or in the earth below—indeed, nothing in all creation will ever be able to separate us from the love of God that is revealed in Christ Jesus our Lord. ~ Romans 8:35-39

"Well, surely he will love me more if I serve him more." Wrong. How can he love us more when he already demonstrated such great love?

Does that mean it is not important for us to serve God? Of course not. But we need to examine our motives. Are we serving him to "earn points"? To motivate him to love us more? Or are we serving him out of our love for him? We love because he first loved us.

Have you hurried up and prayed today? Go ahead and get it done so you can mark it off the list today. Sad but true, that is the case if we treat prayer like a daily activity. Everything about our society has become "quick service" because we fit so much into our day. We run out during our lunch hour to do errands, but we are starting to get a little hungry too. No worries, go through the drive-thru. We get off work and the kids have a game tonight that we need to get to by 6:00... no worries, drive-thru.

Is our prayer becoming a drive-thru? Do we want to make sure to pray every day because "*I need to*"? Or do we pray every day because we *WANT* to? Either way, if we are rushing it, we are missing out on God's grace. It's actually a gift that is given to us.

If we pray just to be praying, how effective is it? Pray like you are face to face with God because if you pray with faith, you are. Pray like you believe He can intervene, and He will lead you. You must believe in what you pray. I had to learn how to pray. I thought that by just closing out everything around me, that was all that was needed. I finally learned to pray as God intended. I would open up my entire everything, heart and mind, and pray. To be honest, I've gone into prayer to just ask for guidance and end up praying for 15-20 minutes and come out bawling like a baby. But coming out of prayer *WITH FAITH* I feel a peace about it like I can't explain. It definitely wasn't what I felt before when my prayer was just me talking.

And my last point today, pray for God's will and plan even when things are going great in your life. Do you have that one friend, or maybe a few, that you only hear from when they need something? You go six months never hearing from this "friend", and then you see his or her name pop up on your phone wanting to borrow a tool or needing a ride, or any number of things. Imagine you being that friend and you dial up God to borrow something. Do we only pray when things are going bad? We have sickness, financial issues, trouble in a relationship... then we pray? God wants to be a full-time friend, not a payday loan. Pray daily for guidance, direction, and wisdom to do all things through Him (Phil 4:13). Pray to say thanks for all He has already done.

When I pray, I start by praising God for who He is, then I move on to the things I'm most thankful for... my salvation, family, friends, job, community anything I have that I'm thankful for. I pray for His protection over these people and things before I ask for guidance or intervention. Don't take anything for granted, be thankful.

Health critics and doctors tell us to avoid drive-thru windows and get in a habit of healthy choices as a lifestyle, not a trend or New Year's resolution. For a healthy relationship and blessed life with Christ, avoid the checklist prayer and believe that your prayer is a face-to-face meeting. Use it as a classroom, asking the great teacher to provide the lessons. You'll be surprised at how much you actually get from it once it's not a task, but instead a welcomed event.

"Therefore, I urge you, brothers and sisters, in view of God's mercy, to offer your bodies as a living sacrifice, holy and pleasing to God—this is your true and proper worship. Do not conform to the pattern of this world, but be transformed by the renewing of your mind. Then you will be able to test and approve what God's will is—his good, pleasing, and perfect will." ~ Romans 12:1-2

The world seems to go faster all the time, and we seem to be busier all the time. If we look at the example Jesus gave us, however, we see swarms of people around him, plenty to keep him busy. He was always in high demand. Yet he took time alone to pray to his Father in heaven, to visit with friends and new acquaintances, and to rest when he had the chance--even amid a storm. Jesus never appeared to be frantic.

When we strive to reach our goals to feel a sense of value and worth, it's easy to get busier and to stress more all the time. We are depending on ourselves. But when we know who we are in Christ and how important we are to him, our outlook on life changes. "Fix your attention on God. You'll be changed from the inside out." Only as you abide in Christ and depend fully on his strength and power . . . only as you choose to focus on him and follow his good plan for your life . . . will you be able to get out of the busyness and stress traps of life. Only then can God bring the best out of you and help you accomplish his purpose for your journey.

Think about some things you can do to reduce the stress in your life. Here are some possibilities to consider:

- Schedule time to read and meditate on God's Word.
- Spend more time being with God--soaking in his presence.
- Journal thoughts that come when you meditate on the Word and talk to him.
- Commit to seeking out a small group fellowship that discusses God's Word and its life application.
- Find time to rest each week.
- Spend quality time with those you care about.

Avoid the drive-thru. Jesus wants to sit with you at the table.

DAY 57 ON THE PORCH

My friends and family—my prayer warriors—played a big role in my healing while battling cancer. It was rough at times, but you fine folks flooded me with messages of kindness. You've offered to bring me things and run errands for me, and some even sent me video links to the gospel according to *Andy Griffith*. That is nothing more than Agape love, which is the unconditional love that Christ has for us. Kindness is a byproduct of that love.

What if kindness — the Jesus kind — covered a world that's so often mean-spirited and calloused toward the needs and feelings of others? I'm not talking about holding doors open or possibly letting someone merge into traffic. Think bigger. Like letting a buddy fish at your favorite spot. What if folks were so kind that it became awkward?

Never mind that some people think kindness is out of vogue for a culture that shouts and cusses at people for leaving pickles on their burgers. Or that kindness is a "cool" word to put on T-shirts and bumper stickers, attempting to get the attention of cruel, apathetic, and brazenly unkind violators, like those who spew hatred toward banana pudding and sweet tea.

We should have this down pat by now. Kindness didn't originate with the Mayberry "be nice" culture, however well-meaning it is. It's been around since the beginning of time. In His divine kindness, God gave us life. In His kindness, He gave us His Spirit's presence here with us and the hope of eternity spent with Him. His kindness takes up residence in us when we accept His kind of love. His kindness exceeds the world's kindness. And according to cable news channels, we've never needed it more.

Kindness is more powerful than most give it credit for. For example, several years ago outside a Dollar General store, I saw kindness break up a fight. Two grown men were so wound up over a parking spot that they used double cuss words. They were ready to roll around right there in the potholes.

A lady, possibly in her seventies, walked close by. Her bag ripped. Purse candy, denture cream, and word-search puzzle books lay scattered on the ground. I went to help her. So did the two prize fighters. They forgot how to be mad at each other and picked up peppermint until the ground was clean. Then they shook hands and talked about the weather. Kindness is that powerful.

Scripture says it is God's kindness that leads us toward repentance. His kindness intends to point us to repentance of sins, to change our inner selves and our old ways of thinking toward His purposes.

Prison ministers tell us that among even hardened inmates, it's often the kindness of Jesus-loving ministers or other people that turns them toward God — not lectures or harshness. Some even had John 3:16 tattooed on their arm right under "MOM".

Anywhere that people are in need of God's love, kindness may open doors that won't budge otherwise. Those doors could be screwed shut with galvanized deck screws and wouldn't stand a chance of holding back God's love. And it starts with kindness. We're talking about kindness that we give to others who may not be able to give anything back, who may not deserve kindness (in our eyes), and who frequently don't thank us for it.

Perhaps a coworker that, no matter what, is always grumpy. Smile and greet them anyway. It may not change their mood, but they'll notice your kindness. And sometimes, that's all it takes to make their day a little better.

But real kindness calls us to look at those who have no defenders. It calls us to welcome the rejected, befriend the friendless, and help all who need it. It tells us to lift the broken, enlarge the small, and favor the weak. Like Jesus did. Like God does.

Tall order! This love is impossible to do by manpower or willpower alone. The Apostle Paul tells us that it is the work of the Holy Spirit within us, reproducing the character of Christ in us that enables this loving kindness.

I've been the beneficiary of others' God-inspired kindness. I've had it thrown at me so hard it left marks. I am forever grateful. I regret the times I could have been kind, but wasn't. Or times I ignored someone's suffering because I couldn't fix it. Or times when my unforgiveness, judgment or apathy kept me from extending kindness to someone.

Solomon instructs us, "Never tire of kindness and loyalty. Hold these virtues tightly. Write them deep within your heart."

Kindness is like snow – it beautifies everything it covers. And it does something else, too. When you extend kindness to others... something amazing happens. Your mouth begins to reshape. You can't stop it. It begins to... smile! It makes you feel good. Our world needs it so much! And it's free for us to give and accept... if we will.

Be the reason someone smiles today.

"Now that I've put you there on a hilltop, on a light stand—shine! Keep open house; be generous with your lives. By opening up to others, you'll prompt people to open up with God, this generous Father in heaven." ~ Matthew 5:16

Being kind can change the world. That's a bold statement. Perhaps we should better say that being kind can change *someone's* world.

It is important that while sharing with others, you do not talk down to them, making them feel as though you are treating them like a child or an inferior person. Your interactions should represent who you are in your walk with Christ. You should have a clear goal of providing insight your friend does not appear to have and moving him or her toward healing. Try to stay at the level of insight relevant to the person's needs.

Freedom from a life-controlling problem is a process. Pray that God will help you disclose all that will assist your friend in that process, but not so much as to produce confusion. And pray that God will use what you say to help set your loved one free.

DAY 58 ON THE PORCH

"Whatcha in for?"

It startled me. I was fully engaged in scrolling through college football lies and tailgate recipes on the great source of knowledge known as Facebook. It sounded more like something I would hear on cell block C. But this place was nowhere near that. It was way worse. Cancer gets discussed here.

Birmingham, Alabama—UAB Kirklin Clinic. The place was full of bald heads and insurance deductibles. The god-awful smell of disinfectant was everywhere. This is where all of us come when we are going through a cuss-word diagnosis. I put down my phone and looked up. He was frail. His button-up shirt was three sizes too big. It probably fit perfectly just a few trips ago.

"Pre-op appointment," I answered. "They're gonna unzip me again this Friday."

"Cancer?" He asked.

"Yep."

"The bad kind?"

"Is there any other?"

"What are they calling yours?" He questioned.

"Take your pick," I tell him. "Melanoma started all this mess. It got mad and attacked my lymph nodes. Had a surgery or four. Been doing treatments. Popped up in my kidney now. Left side. They say this one is renal cell carcinoma. More lymph nodes coming out with it."

"Dang it, son," he says shaking his head. "You a show-off ain't ya?"

"Go big or go home," I say through a smile. "What about you? What'd they sentence you for?"

"They got me with neuroblastoma. Caught red-handed."

I had to Google it... and Good-God! If you don't know what that is, think of the worst cancer imaginable. Then triple it. Then, multiply it by sheer terror. Carry the two. Divide by financial crippling. And that's before it gets bad.

His treatment folder reads like an unabridged Chinese dictionary. Drill a port in his chest, four rounds of chemo, invasive surgery, radiation, months of immunotherapy, scans, so much blood work you can't hold water. Like I said—cuss words.

He shifts himself. It's obvious that he is fighting pain. "They've been cutting on me since day one. Almost haven't got anything left to take. But they can't take this away."

He points to his narrow face. His smile is so big I squint from the glare. I can relate. I use mine as well. I have been holding onto my smile for months now. Some days it's forced. But afterward, I feel better.

I haven't had a good night's sleep in a month of Sundays. I feel like I'm at one of the UAB campuses more than I'm at home. I get tired from doing anything. I have to take a nap just from laughing too hard. And I get so worked up that all I have left that goes right are my cheek muscles. So, I use them to smile. And I do it often. I guess I'm afraid it will leave, too. So, I'm using it while I can.

It's been hard. I won't sugarcoat it. Some days are worse than others. Don't get me wrong. Every day is a blessing. I absolutely love life. But if I wasn't walking with God, this would be like bench pressing a cement truck.

But it makes it even harder with two kids. Trying to tell them as much as you can without their world falling apart... that's tough. They know everything, but I just really don't want them to realize what's happening. I worry more about them and my wife than I do me. They're the ones that are affected by this. It's like secondhand cancer.

But as I sit here waiting for my name to get called so they can swipe the paint off my debit card, I realize that I don't have it so bad. There are folks way worse than me. I see kids with bald heads waiting also. Some have on ball caps. A little girl is playing with her Barbie. She has shaved Barbie's head also. One little boy has on a Spider-Man costume—the whole thing... socks, mask... everything... complete with a web shooter.

I watch as I wait. I'm mesmerized by kids with smiles and mommas without. Another little girl sits in her mom's lap. She's scared to move. A boy, maybe ten at the most, has on a baseball cap. I imagined he loved playing baseball. I bet he was great... when he could play. But cancer robbed that from him.

Spider-Man is making noises that I guess are what a web shooter makes. He's hitting everybody with make-believe webs. I get nailed... twice. I smile at Spidey. He smiles back. I can't see his mouth, but his eyes are smiling so hard that his face may stick like that.

Those eyes. Those little, hopeful eyes. They did something to me. They did something to my eyes. They fogged up like I had top-shelf cataracts. Then the dam broke. My emotions ran down my face soaked my germ mask.

I had a pocket full of "God Is Bigger" bracelets. I take these with me everywhere. They all got one. Everyone in the room. Mommas and daddies included. Spidey got two.

It's not fair, dadgummit. I've done some crappy things in my life. I've driven seventy in a fifty-five. I cheated in algebra class. I eat fried foods and tell my doctor I have no idea why my cholesterol is up. I have taken every tag off every mattress I've ever owned. I don't like this awful thing, but I can understand why I've got this cuss word growing in me. I guess it's payback for all the things I didn't do right. But these kids... they haven't had a chance to screw up yet.

Each day, forty-seven kids are diagnosed with cancer in this country. I looked it up. Sitting right there today getting hit by invisible spiderwebs, I saw the statistics. That's approximately seventeen thousand kids each year. How's that fair?

The good news is that eighty-four percent of those kids will be cured. The bad news is: that you never know for certain whether your kid will be in that eighty-four percent. You can't relax. Twenty-four hours per day, you're afraid. You learn never to trust good news, you learn to never—NEVER—get your hopes up. Prayer is your full-time job. But somehow, some way... you can always smile.

Look, I'm good with my diagnosis. I'm perfectly okay with it. I found peace in a place where it should be extinct. Doctors told me to get ready for a long, rough ride. I told them to get ready for a great big miracle.

I'm in this for something bigger than myself. It's bigger than just beating the stew out of this cuss word. It's about Him. It's about my God.

I have said before: I didn't "get cancer." Instead, God *"ALLOWED me to use cancer"* to glorify Him. I wouldn't say I was chosen for this, but I will take the job. And I'm trying like my life depends on it, because.... well.

I could say at the end of this, when I beat it, that I will have a humdinger of a testimony. That may be the case. But why wait? Why can't I use this to tell others about how great God is now? What's wrong with shouting from the rooftops today? It's easy to shout glory to Him after you've beat cancer. It's easy to talk about great things when things are... well, going great. But I want to stand in the fire, laugh in the devil's face, and sing God's praises.

I want to tell others about how great He has been to me, all while hooked up to chemicals that glow and cause me to hurt all over. Because what he endured for me can't even be compared to how little I can do for Him. And on the days that I hurt really bad. On the days I feel defeated. On the days that rank right up there next to getting hit by a full-grown garbage truck, I want to smile and tell others that God is bigger.

A skinny little man who's fighting for his life once smiled at me and told me that nothing could take his smile away. I gave him one of my bracelets and told him that God wouldn't let them if they tried.

And I wished like the dickens that the little man would ask me that question again: "Whatcha in for?" I think I would have a different answer now that I've had a chance to think about it.

It's rather simple. "I'm in it for God... I'm in it for eternity."
"Trust God from the bottom of your heart; don't try to figure

out everything on your own. Listen for God's voice in everything you do, everywhere you go; he's the one who will keep you on track. Don't assume that you know it all. Run to God! Run from evil! Your body will glow with health, your very bones will vibrate with life!" ~ Proverbs 3:5-8

God has planned for each of us to enjoy self-worth, security, and a sense of belonging—things we can only experience as we learn to trust him. Life brings challenges, but God does not intend for us to have to face those challenges alone.

No matter what your circumstances No matter what you have done or what you are feeling inside God loves you and is waiting for you to trust him—and to be willing to do things his way. You'll soon learn that his way is always the best way.

DAY 59 ON THE PORCH

Some days are hard. I am not talking about hard as in long-term illnesses, mental disabilities, or financial ruin from late-night internet shopping. I am talking about just the fatigue that sometimes comes from our day-to-day schedules. Like some days, I feel like I watched the world come alive early in the morning… and eight weeks later, the sun finally sets. There are Buicks made in the seventies that are getting better gas mileage than me some days.

Lately, most days are long for me. I'm finally starting to admit that I do have limitations. I once could go two straight days on a single peanut butter sandwich and water from a hose pipe. I need to mention that during this era, my main transportation was a bicycle, and my cowlick was more evident.

But things changed. Over time, my days got longer, and I needed more peanut butter sandwiches. A cuss word was found in my body. It has been proven that even when you have the best outlook on life, you're still vulnerable.

As of lately, I've thought a lot about those childhood days. I've recalled how great it was. I had friends that were tougher than boot leather, and most of the time, we all smelled like it as well. We would stay out all day. We had not heard of the word "tired". I think it got invented right around the time we figured out what employment was.

We would come home after a long day with just as much energy as we left with. You didn't have to tell us to be home, we knew. But between the leaving and the arriving, we lived our best lives. The woods behind an old sewing plant in my hometown were our playground. The things I could tell you about those woods are legendary. They were home to the remains of old houses, abandoned appliances, and creeks loaded with enough crawdads to feed a busload of Cajuns.

And after we explored every square inch of those woods, we would make our way home. At the time, we had no idea how much we would later be thankful for those days. At the end of every day, we were blessed more than a seagull with a French fry... and we didn't even know it.

I've always been thankful for every morning God gives me, but at the end of those days, man, that's where it was at. Even now, I'm extremely grateful for them. But even as much as those days mean to me, the end of the day is what fuels my drive to serve God. At the end of the day, God will always be the source of my strength. He's better than two peanut butter sandwiches and an RC Cola after a bike ride.

He'll always be the source of hope that gets me through the toughest times. I have no idea what my future holds. Not long ago, I wondered if I even had a future. I knew I should be worried about the news that doctors once gave me, but for some reason, I wasn't.

Perhaps it's because I'm not smart enough to understand how serious it was. Maybe I've been through so much already, that I've grown numb to bad news. But maybe, it's because I know He'll always be the source of courage that makes me want to get up in the morning and try again or try harder. He'll always be the source of light when the road is dark and unclear.

At the end of the day, God will always be the source of my optimism because I have faith in him. I have faith in his plans and his justice. I have had more body parts removed than a demolition derby car, but I trust that this is just part of a divine weight loss plan.

At the end of the day, I have faith in his lessons and his timing. I have faith in his losses and his blessings. I have faith in his guidance and in the path He chose for me. I have faith in his mercy and his miracles.

Miracles. That word keeps coming up. And at the end of the day, I still believe in them. I do. I really, really do. I have faith in God because every time I lost hope, He blessed me with something to be grateful for, and every time I thought He was punishing me, he was actually releasing me from a poisonous cycle.

And every time I felt dead inside, He brought me back to life and gave me a passion for what I believe in. At the end of the day, God will always be the source of my comfort. I find comfort in my family, my friends, my cousins, my work, and the people I love but I know that everything can change in the blink of an eye.

A surgery could go bad. The doctor's plans could change. My cable could go out, or for Heaven's sake, Alabama should fail to make the college football playoffs. Lord help us if that happens. But I know that no matter how solid everything seems, it can easily dissolve... everything except for God and His love for me. For you. For us all. That will never change.

Too many people in my life have been taken, but my faith in my Savior remains solid. He's the only constant in my life. I can lean on Him without the fear that He'd change or let me down. At the end of the day, God will always be the reason behind every success, every achievement, and every obstacle I overcome.

He's the reason behind these horrible renditions of words. And I pray daily that somehow, He finds a way to use these words to help someone else. I don't know how that works... but He does, and that's good enough for me.

At the end of the day, God will always be the source of my happiness. My beautiful wife and wonderful children make me full of love and happiness, but I know that it is through Him that I share life with them.

When He listens to my prayers and answers them... When He redirects me to an even better destination than the one I had in mind... When He pushes me to bring out my talent, my strength, or my resilience every time I'm close to giving up.

When He nudges me to wake up and walk away from toxic people...When He helps me detach from the things that are not meant for me... my faith strengthens.

At the end of the day, God will always be the source of my strength because He's the only one who hears my most terrifying thoughts and calms me down and He's the only one who reads my mind and knows what's in my heart and somehow eases them.

At the end of the day, God is always with me through the darkest and most painful times, I know He won't abandon me and that gives me all the strength I need to power through, and it makes me unafraid of falling because He will always be right there to pick me up.

At the end of the day, I'm glad that I am a child of God.

"But we must keep going in the direction that we are now headed." ~ Philippians 3:16

It is important to acknowledge any life-controlling problem in your life, admitting it to God and to yourself, asking him for forgiveness and help, accepting responsibility, sharing your struggle with a friend, and preparing to move on. Then begins the process of walking out the changes—to keep going in the direction that you are now headed.

These changes may involve steps like stopping the use of alcohol, drugs or pornography, ending an unhealthy relationship, reordering priorities, becoming accountable to a support group, and going to church regularly. The negative behavior caused by your problem may have destroyed your self-esteem. You might still be dealing with anger, fear, and shame.

As you begin to walk out the changes in your life and to see yourself as God's special creation, it is vital that you walk in agreement with God. Agreement that He has forgiven you, and He can, and will, deliver you from what is meant to harm you. Agreement that He will give you the strength you need. Agreement that He created you for a positive purpose and will help you accomplish that purpose. Agreement that you will submit to Him and put Him first in all you do. Agreement that He loves you and will be with you through every trial, through every circumstance, through every difficult step—and that with his help, you can do it. ***"Christ gives me the strength to face anything." ~ Philippians 4:13***

DAY 60 ON THE PORCH

My home church hosted a wild game feast and outdoor extravaganza not long ago. Folks from all over the state have been lured here to eat seasoned, exotic roadkill. It has been said that you can lure a man anywhere if you put food in front of him. As a Baptist, I can confirm this.

I remember the first time I ate wild game. It was at a family reunion. My Uncle Bill had prepared a thick gravy with an unknown meat ingredient. After consuming two large bowls, he laughed and said, "Never knew you liked armadillo."

I almost threw up. Up until this point, the most feral thing I had ever eaten was my cousin Ed's prize-fighting rooster after he'd lost a match against a Rhode Island Red. But Uncle Bill eventually came clean. He was just joking. He'd never serve us anything like armadillo. This meal was more highfalutin than that. Luckily for us, this mystery meat turned out to only be possum.

"Good for your cholesterol," said Bill.

But at this hootenanny at our church, it was much more than what you'd find on a two-lane Alabama road. Here, hunters and outdoor lovers of all stripes have built perhaps the only chance in the Western Hemisphere to try some exotic game meat from land and sea that most restaurants won't touch: raccoon, squirrel, pheasant, speckled-belly goose, rabbit, venison, duck, quail, hippopotamus kneecaps, and more. This isn't your average church potluck.

There's a tradition among outdoorsmen and hunters to spend time together around a meal. They prepare meals that take all day to cook, which will get them out of yard work and honey-do lists. They take great pride in this. They refuse to go to some dining establishment and pay upwards of sixty dollars for a good steak.

No siree Bob! Instead, they buy precision-sighted rifles, fifty-thousand-dollar ATVs, and high-tech clothes that smell like a whitetail doe looking for a boyfriend. They'll lease land, pay fees, and wake up at midnight to go sit in Wi-Fi-equipped heated shooting boxes. Whereas they will bring home food for the table that the wife refuses to eat. That'll teach these restaurants a thing or two!

But we were there for more than over-salted tenderloin and monthly fees. We were there to celebrate all of God's creations and show off Italian imported scopes that can zoom in on a squirrel eight hundred miles away.

"It taps into that manly tradition by providing a place for people to talk about their adventures and their love for the outdoors and eat some good food," says the event organizer. "And it gets them into church."

What better place to lie about the one that got away?

Our guest speaker is professional bass fisherman, Clay Dyer, someone I've known for years. I first met him at the recreational center in Hamilton, Alabama when I was a teenager. My buddies and I would go there to play basketball, and Clay would be set up on a small goal on the side of the court. Watching him shoot a basketball was better than a Harlem Globetrotter episode. He hardly ever missed.

When I arrived tonight, Clay and I reminisced about the olden days. He poked fun at how his Hamilton Aggies always whipped up on my Brilliant Tigers, and I accused him of having a bad memory and paying off referees. He talked about his coaching days, and I told him how I could still hit a free throw if given unlimited tries, and motivation such as a bite of banana pudding for every shot made.

But it wasn't long before our conversation turned away from our glory days, and toward something else. The real reason he was here—Faith, God, and overcoming obstacles in our lives.

Clay is not your average outdoorsman. He was born without legs and only one partial arm with no fingers or thumb. Yet, Clay has never let these obstacles stop him. In fact, he has excelled. He can do more than most people born with all their parts. He uses his neck and arm to hold and cast his fishing rod. He attaches lures using his mouth. I would be plum embarrassed matching my fishing skills up to his.

"I was born the way you see me now, with no legs past the hip and half a right arm. My mom never consumed drugs, that would've been a medical reason I was born this way, so what I like to tell people now is that it was an act of God, and I wouldn't have it any other way," said Clay to folks gathered to hear his story.

Now he competes on the national pro fishing circuit, and he's won multiple state and regional fishing tournaments. He has more sponsors than Rocky Balboa and has become known as the most inspirational fisherman on the planet.

"In my life, I'd have to say the biggest lesson that God's taught me is the value of patience," Clay says. "The value of determination and willpower, you know, but yet to allow God to guide and direct me and follow His lead."

Even with these obstacles, Clay has always managed to have an upbeat attitude. He only remembers one time when he questioned why God had made him this way.

"When I was still a small kid, I said, 'Daddy, why did God make me like this?' My dad looked me square in the eyes and said, 'Son, I don't know, but I know God doesn't make mistakes.' When I look back on it, I realize that I didn't see it at the time, but God knew when He made me, He made me for a purpose to be able to go out and witness and encourage people to live for Him."

I think of my own situations. My life has not been all cupcakes and ten-pound bass, either. I grew up without most of the things kids had. We survived on a limited income inside public housing. I've had things happen that I've never told anyone about. Things that should have broken me. But hearing Clay talk about how blessed he is makes my life look like I was raised by royalty.

Before we left, I signed some of my books for him. We talked about his own book. We each admitted that two old Marion County, Alabama boys shouldn't have been able to get to where we are in life. We've had too many things try to beat us down. But here we are. All because of the same thing— God's Grace.

"Let me pay you for these books. Make a donation... something," he insisted. I sternly refused.

What Clay is doing is payment enough. He's inspiring thousands. He's telling them that life is beautiful and when God is leading you through this journey, it's going to be amazing... every aspect of it. Even the mountains he places in front of you.

I left the event thinking about that. I sat in my truck for a few minutes before leaving. I have been given a platform that I never imagined I'd have. I've been able to holler until my lungs collapse about how big my God is. My books have sold more copies than I ever imagined. I can barely form sentences, but somehow, I am being booked weekly to speak at universities, churches, conventions, and Baptist potlucks. In my eyes, this should never be happening. But God...

As I sat in my truck, I thought back to a couple of years ago. The day I learned cancer had found me. "God, I can't figure out what You're doing!" I pleaded. "Why? I'm faithful. I'm obedient. I'm doing what You ask. This has to be a mistake, God. It has to be!"

The journey began to look different than I'd imagined. Multiple surgeries. A cancer that kept spreading. The road was filled with more potholes than I'd anticipated, and as I let God direct my steps, it seemed He was leading me to the middle of nowhere, rather than in the direction of a promise fulfilled. I didn't doubt God's presence, but I questioned His plans.

On my good days, I felt optimistic and persistent. On my bad days, I felt angry and confused. And on that evening when a phone call sank my hope, I felt helpless and stuck. I remember wondering why. But somewhere, deep inside, I knew that God would use this, not only to allow me to grow closer to Him but to also minister to others that were struggling.

But still... "Could You just show me what You're doing, Lord?" I begged.

I don't know how long I sat there and waited for the Lord's reply. But I do know there was no flash of lightning illuminating God's brilliant plan. No thundering voice explaining His mystifying methods. Just a quiet thought impressed upon my haggard heart: **"Do you want a God you can explain or a God you can extol?"**

Suddenly, through my haze of fear, I recognized an uncomfortable truth: A God of infinite majesty can't be measured. A God who unleashes miracles can't be contained. A God whose love is eternal can't be explained.

As I left that wild game expo, I think I finally figured out that my cancer journey had been in the works for fifty years. Before I was born, God knew what He would do through this. And it's pretty evident. What my buddy told us, really is all we need to know... **God doesn't make mistakes.**

"I am the LORD, the God of all mankind. Is anything too hard for me?"~ Jeremiah 32:27

When we are facing difficult times, sometimes we begin to feel as though our situation is hopeless. If friends and family try to encourage us, we might respond with, "But you don't understand."

Our loved ones might or might not understand, but the Lord always understands. He always cares. And he assures us that nothing is too hard for him.

What challenges are you facing? An illness? A rebellious child? Marriage problems? Financial challenges? Whatever it is, remember that God is bigger.

As you turn your problem over to God, remember that his answer might not be what you are expecting. And his timing might seem ever so slow. But he will be with you throughout the process. And his plan ... and his time ... are always the best plan and the best time. No matter how things appear right now, he will work all things together for good. He loves you ... and nothing is too hard for him.

EPILOGUE

Don't stop now! Dig deeper! Sixty days is just the beginning. Keep going. Develop a routine that makes you thirst for your time with God. Having a deeply personal relationship with God is exciting – it brings a lot of security and confidence as we try to grow.

However, it does require us to explore the deeper parts of our hearts that may be uncomfortable to examine and be honest about with ourselves and with God. But the outcome is immeasurable considering what it can do to unlock our true potential.

I can tell the difference in my times with God when I'm just going through the motions and when I'm really present, engaged, and interacting with scriptures and in prayer. When it's the latter, my heart is more receptive, I get new insights from the Bible, and I feel God's presence in my life.

Unfortunately, I do not so readily invite God's "searching gaze into my heart." I'm afraid that if I slow down enough, I'm going to end up seeing and feeling things that are painful, difficult, or shameful. It feels as if once I reflect and acknowledge some deeper truth, it will become final and definitive about who I am. So, for most of my life, I lived pretty aloof, ignoring any emotions or guilt I would feel along the way, and if I felt anything negative, I just slept it off and tried to forget it.

I never slowed down enough to understand why and where the anger was coming from, or the feelings of fear and embarrassment that simmered underneath. My busy and demanding lifestyle just caused more setbacks in my already distant relationship with God. At times, the moments I spent with God seemed more like I was pleading for his intervention, more than me wanting to grow closer.

However, reflecting on our whys and allowing God to search our innermost thoughts and desires is how we can deepen our walk with God, understand why we do what we do through the scriptures, and allow God to help us become who we are meant to be as we reflect and grow.

Knowing that God is with us every step of the way and guiding us in the best direction helps make discovering new truths about ourselves an exciting journey! Holding onto scriptures reminds me of God's presence in my life and helps me feel safe as I see where God is trying to take me.

When I saw that God had a much better plan and purpose for my life, then it didn't matter how difficult the truths about where I was really at were, because God had the power and desire to redirect my life.

So, don't stop here. Spend more and more time on God's porch. He will awaken something in you that you never knew existed.

ALSO BY RUSSELL L. ESTES

Southern Roots: Lessons From a Southern Upbringing

When the Lights Go Out

God is Bigger: Than the Mountain You Are Facing